Cross-Country Skiing
Yellowstone
Country

by
Ken and Dena Olsen
Steve and Hazel Scharosch

You may order extra copies of this book by writing Abacus Enterprises, P.O. Box 9035, Casper, WY 82609. Phone: (307) 235-1829. Or call Falcon Press. Phone: (800) 582-2665.

Library of Congress Catalog Card Number: 92-85241
ISBN 1-56044-191-7

Copyright © 1992 by
Ken and Dena Olsen
Steve and Hazel Scharosch

Acknowledgements

Cross-Country Skiing Yellowstone Country owes its beginning to Susan Bowland of West Yellowstone, Montana, who encouraged us to come back and try the skiing as we passed through one October. We returned, and have come back every winter since, because this is grand country and the people are wonderful. This book is an outgrowth of our love for the area.

We owe an enormous amount to Kristen Moulton and my mother, Kay Olsen, for their patient editing. They are both gifted writers, and that made this all the much easier.

Falcon Press provided valuable publication support.

Several people from the National Park Service, U.S. Forest Service, Harriman State Park and the Rendezvous Ski Trail System gave generously in helping make sure this book was accurate and up-to-date. They include Drew Barney, Colette Daigle-Berg, Norm Bishop, Ed Brashier, Gene Hardin, Les Inafuku, Rick McAdam, Brian O'dea, Bundy Phillips, and many others.

–Ken Olsen

Contents

Trails

Introduction

From Heart Attack Hill to Old Faithful, Yellowstone country is unbeatable when covered with snow. Winter visitors have an advantage in Yellowstone National Park. A small fraction of the more than 3 million visitors who come to the nation's oldest national park do it in winter, leaving the buffalo, elk, moose, swans, stunning mountains and crisp solitude of the ski trail to the winter adventurer.

Not only do you avoid bumper-to-bumper crowds, you can enjoy the best cross-country skiing in the Northwest. Annual snowfall varies from an average of 80 inches at Mammoth Hot Springs to 164 inches at West Yellowstone, Montana. An average of 30 inches is on the ground during the winter season—officially mid-December to mid-March.

Yellowstone has hosted skiers for more than a century. One of the first made it to Mammoth Hot Springs in 1873. The U.S. Cavalry later used skis on anti-poacher patrols. Olympic skiers from the United States and Norway have trained here, but for most of the winter, these trails are barely visited. Most people come to snowmobile or visit Old Faithful by snowcoach and seldom leave the heavily traveled paths to see a more natural side of Yellowstone.

Two excellent ski-trail systems are found at West Yellowstone, right next to the national park. And Old Faithful is the center of a trail system you can reach by snowcoach, for a fee.

Other spectacular ski trails are a maximum 35-mile drive from West Yellowstone. Harriman State Park sees only 6,000 skiers from Thanksgiving to April yet boasts a magnificent waterfowl refuge, trails through a historic ranch, and challenging routes like the Ridge Loop that traverses Heart Attack Hill and Coronary Bypass.

Skiers can rent a cabin on the banks of the Buffalo River and take the Moose Loop and other trails. This area offers swans, moose, the Tetons as a backdrop and a beautiful river kept flowing year-round by hot springs.

Northern Yellowstone National Park has more challenging skiing. The trails are often longer and, in some cases, the terrain is tougher. But the scenery, solitude and solace are equally appealing and there is great variety. You can enjoy a short ski around the thermal features of Mammoth Hot Springs or enjoy the broad vistas of the Blacktail Plateau near Tower Junction.

The sun almost always shines in this country and the wind rarely blows. The mercury often tops out at 20 or 30 degrees, but one can ski comfortably at 10 degrees below zero without bulky arctic clothing. The cool temperatures mean better snow conditions, better skiing.

Four skiers with a range of experience took great pleasure in preparing this guide. This book takes you to all of the public trails in Yellowstone National Park and those within 30 miles of West Yellowstone, Montana. It categorizes trails according to difficulty, gives elevation profiles so you can judge the terrain and tells you a bit about the scenery and wildlife.

This guide also tells you where you will have to pay to ski, where you can ski for free and how often trails are groomed. From trail length to how to get there, we give you the most complete guide to some of America's best cross-country skiing.

–Ken Olsen

How To Use This Guide

The map on the following page shows the ski trail systems covered by this guide.

Each chapter of this guide covers a geographic area. Within each chapter, a general area overview is provided, followed by the trail descriptions. Trails are grouped by trail system and then by difficulty. The ratings in this guide do not always correspond with the ratings the government agencies give these trails. We have given more weight to trail length and have tried to consider the casual skier in developing our ratings.

Here's how to understand the ratings:

Rating	Symbol	Description
Easy		Trails less than 5 miles long with gentle topography. Beginning skiers with limited experience can generally negotiate these trails. Level terrain will require use of the basic diagonal stride; downhill sections may require snowplowing; uphill sections may require use of side steps or herringbone.
Moderate		Trails less than 10 miles long with varied terrain. Skiers should be able to negotiate turns using snowplow, telemark or step turns. Uphill stretches require use of herringbone or side steps.
Difficult		Trails with difficult terrain, or trails more than 10 miles long. Turns require proficiency in snowplowing, telemarking or step turning as the curves are frequently sharp with little room to negotiate. Steep downhill runs require many quick turns. Uphill grades are steep and require use of herringbone.
Extreme		Trails with difficult terrain, coupled with remote locations, dangerous off-trail conditions, or other potential hazards. Turns require proficiency in snowplowing, telemarking or step turning as the curves are frequently sharp with little room to negotiate. Steep downhill runs require many quick turns; otherwise you may collide with trees or rocks. Uphill grades are steep and require use of herringbone. Climbing skins may be required. Avalanche danger may be present. Skiers should check on local snow conditions before attempting these trails.

Map of Trail Systems Covered in this Guide

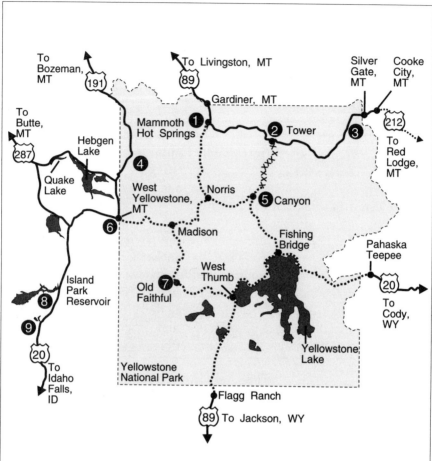

Legend

`------` Yellowstone Park Boundary	❶ Mammoth Hot Springs
─── Roads/highways open to automobile traffic during winter season	❷ Tower
`........` Roads/highways open to oversnow vehicles only during winter season	❸ Northeast Yellowstone
`xxxxx` Roads/highways closed to both automobiles and oversnow vehicles during winter season	❹ Fir Ridge
	❺ Canyon
	❻ West Yellowstone
	❼ Old Faithful
	❽ Brimstone/Buffalo River
	❾ Harriman State Park

⊢————⊣ 10 miles

Ⓝ

Winter Safety

Even the most experienced skiers find themselves in life-threatening situations because of injury, accident, over-exertion, broken equipment or rapidly changing weather.

These cautions can help you avoid most winter mishaps and deal with those you can't avoid:

Winter Safety Cautions

- Tell someone where you're going and when you plan to return. Contact them when you return.
- Ski with at least one friend.
- Check the weather forecast, avalanche possibility and trail conditions before starting your trip. Avalanches are most common when heavy, wet snow falls on top of older, dry and unstable snow.
- Flesh freezes easily at 10 degrees below zero. You also can freeze your ears, face, hands and feet while skiing downhill or skiing in even a light breeze. Carry a windbreaker and other wind clothing. The following chart shows the cooling effect of even a slight breeze.

Wind Chill Chart

Wind Speed	Temperature (Fahrenheit)															
Calm	35	30	25	20	15	10	5	0	-5	-10	-15	-20	-25	-30	-35	-40
	Equivalent Wind Chill Temperature															
5 mph	33	27	21	16	12	7	1	-6	-11	-15	-20	-26	-31	-35	-41	-47
10 mph	21	16	9	2	-2	-9	-15	-22	-27	-31	-38	-45	-52	-58	-64	-70
15 mph	16	11	1	-6	-11	-18	-25	-33	-40	-45	-51	-60	-65	-70	-78	-85
20 mph	12	3	-4	-9	-17	-24	-32	-40	-46	-52	-60	-68	-76	-81	-88	-96
25 mph	7	0	-7	-15	-22	-29	-37	-45	-52	-58	-67	-75	-83	-89	-96	-104
30 mph	5	-2	-11	-18	-26	-33	-41	-49	-56	-63	-70	-78	-87	-94	-101	-109
35 mph	3	-4	-13	-20	-27	-35	-43	-52	-60	-67	-72	-83	-90	-98	-105	-113
40 mph	1	-4	-15	-22	-29	-36	-45	-54	-62	-69	-76	-87	-94	-101	-107	-116

Exposed flesh may freeze within 1 minute   Exposed flesh may freeze within 30 seconds

- Choose outings that are appropriate for your group's skill and physical abilities. Pace yourself. Don't wait until you're tired to turn back.
- Dress appropriately, using multiple layers of thin clothing. This will allow you to add or remove clothing to prevent chilling or overheating. Avoid tight-fitting clothes that restrict body movement or blood circulation. Select clothes made of wool or specialized synthetics (polypropylene, for example) that wick away perspiration and retain their insulating value when wet. Avoid cotton garments—they hold moisture against your skin. Take a warm hat—most body heat is lost through your head. For extreme weather conditions take a face mask or balaclava-type hat. Sunscreen and sunglasses are musts because sunburn and snowblindness are common risks on the high-altitude Yellowstone Plateau. Wear stout ski boots with thick wool socks and waterproof gaiters, particularly if you are skiing in soft powder snow or on ungroomed trails.
- Use caution on icy boardwalks and walkways. On several ski trails in Yellowstone National Park, skiers use the same boardwalks and walkways that summer hikers use. These boardwalks and walkways are often ice-covered and slick. We recommend you take your skis off and walk across the icy sections.
- Stay on designated trails when viewing Yellowstone's geysers, hot pools and other thermal wonders. They are breathtaking when viewed from a safe distance. This beauty masks the danger of injury or death for those who venture too close. Many of Yellowstone's thermal pools are ringed by thin, delicate crusts covering waters near or above the boiling point. Established boardwalks and trails serve the dual purpose of protecting visitors from parboiling themselves while preserving delicate thermal formations. Don't defeat their purpose.
- Keep your distance from wildlife, for your sake and theirs. Studies show that skiers displace elk and buffalo more than snowmobilers. Moreover, wild animals may react unpredictably when they feel threatened by an approaching skier. If you encounter buffalo, moose or elk on a ski trail, wait for them to move away, or make a wide detour. Be particularly wary of buffalo, moose or elk with young. These animals may go to any length to protect their young. Do not pursue wildlife for photos because this causes them to waste valuable energy that helps them survive hostile Yellowstone winters. Park regulations require that you keep at least 100 yards from bears, 25 yards from all other wildlife.
- Trail signs provide information to help you enjoy skiing. Pay particu-

lar attention to signs warning of steep hills, one-way skier flow, avalanche hazards, closed trails or wildlife danger.

- Avoid skiing on frozen lakes. Due to the thermal activity on the Yellowstone Plateau, lakes often have patches of thin ice caused by hot springs and water currents. These thin patches aren't easily seen until it's too late.

    Overflow—standing water and slush on top of the ice—also is a danger on frozen lakes. Skiing through a patch of overflow can result in wet feet, which greatly increases the chance of frostbite. Overflow also causes ice to form on the bottom of your skis, making them unusable.

    Dogs usually are not allowed on groomed trails. If you are taking your dog on off-trail ski trips, make sure the dog stays clear of frozen lakes. Skiers have lost pets through the ice in the Yellowstone area.

- Recognize the warning signs of frostbite and hypothermia*—know how to treat both:

    Frostbite is caused by ice crystals forming in the skin tissue; appearing as white or yellowish patches. Wrap the victim in blankets or clothing and give warm drinks. Avoid alcohol, caffeine, nicotine and tranquilizers as these substances disrupt the circulation system and can aggravate the situation. If possible, immerse frostbitten skin in *warm* water. *Never* rub frostbitten skin with snow. If there is any possibility the affected area will refreeze after thawing, do not thaw.

    Hypothermia is where your internal body temperature drops well-below normal. It is caused by body heat being lost faster than you can produce it. If heat loss is unchecked, energy reserves become exhausted and internal body temperature begins to plummet, resulting in stupor, collapse and death.

    Hypothermia is typically caused by a combination of exposure and exhaustion, not bitter cold. In fact, most hypothermia cases develop in air temperatures between +30 and +50 degrees because people underestimate the danger of over-exertion and chilling at such temperatures. Hypothermia is the number-one killer of outdoor recreationists.

    The first signs of hypothermia appear as the brain temperature is lowered, resulting in a loss of judgment and reasoning. Common symptoms are uncontrollable fits of shivering; vague, slow, slurred speech; memory lapses, incoherence; immobile, fumbling hands; frequent stumbling; a lurching gait; drowsiness (sleeping at this point

---

* Much of the information on hypothermia was paraphrased from: Winter Recreation Safety Guide. USDA Forest Service in cooperation with the US Ski Association. Program Aid No. 1140.

is fatal); exhaustion; inability to get up after a rest.

A hypothermia victim may deny he or she is in trouble. Believe the symptoms, not the victim. Even mild symptoms demand immediate, drastic treatment.

If you suspect someone is suffering from hypothermia:

- Get victim out of the wind and rain or snow.
- Remove all wet clothes.
- If the patient is only mildly impaired:
  - Give warm drinks.
  - Get person into warm clothes and warm sleeping bag.
  - Avoid alcohol, caffeine, nicotine, tranquilizers and other substances that affect circulation.
- If patient is semi-conscious or worse:
  - Try to keep them awake; give them warm drinks.
  - Leave person stripped. Put victim in sleeping bag with another person, also naked. If you have a double bag, put the victim between two warm, naked people. *Skin-to-skin* contact is the most effective treatment.
  - Build a fire to help warm the victim.
  - Concentrate heat on the trunk of the body first, that is the shoulders, chest, and stomach. Keep the head low and feet up to get warm blood circulating to the head. Keep the person quiet; do not jostle, massage or rub.
  - Avoid alcohol, caffeine, nicotine, tranquilizers and other substances that affect circulation.

Of course, the best treatment for hypothermia is prevention. The time to prevent hypothermia is during exposure and gradual exhaustion. Moisture and wind increase your rate of heat loss tremendously. Avoid both. Find protection from adverse weather, conserve your energy and don't exhaust yourself.

Checklist of Equipment

Basic:

- ❑ Your own copy of this book!
- ❑ Skis, poles, and boots
- ❑ Ski wax, scraper, and cork if using waxable skis
- ❑ Spare ski tip
- ❑ Basic repair tools: screwdriver, pliers
- ❑ Pocket knife
- ❑ Compass
- ❑ First aid kit
- ❑ Sun block, lip balm
- ❑ Toilet paper
- ❑ Water bottle
- ❑ High-energy ready-to-eat food (dried fruit, jerky, nuts, candy)
- ❑ Metal cup, suitable for melting snow in
- ❑ Maps
- ❑ Matches or lighter and candle or firestarter
- ❑ Flashlight with extra bulb and batteries
- ❑ Warm hat (balaclava or face mask for extreme weather)
- ❑ Warm mittens or gloves
- ❑ Thermal underwear (wool or polypropylene)
- ❑ Warm pants or knickers
- ❑ Sweater or heavy shirt (wool)
- ❑ Coat
- ❑ Waterproof/windproof shell pants and jacket
- ❑ Spare socks, mittens, and hat
- ❑ Gaiters
- ❑ Sunglasses
- ❑ Foil blanket (Space blanket)

Advanced:

- ❑ Goggles for wind-blown snow
- ❑ Climbing skins
- ❑ Shovel for digging shelter
- ❑ Extra coat
- ❑ Avalanche cord or beacon

Optional:

- ❑ Binoculars
- ❑ Camera & lenses, film
- ❑ Hand towel

Trail Courtesy

A bit of thoughtfulness makes skiing more pleasant for everyone.

- Don't walk in the ski tracks without skis. Don't snowshoe in the ski tracks.
- Yield the right-of-way to downhill skiers.
- Keep to your right on the trail. If there is more than one groomed track, ski in the right-hand track except when passing.
- Step off the trail or out of the tracks when taking a break for a photo, snacks or to chat.
- Don't ski two or three abreast if it blocks the trail, especially in steep sections or where visibility is limited.
- Only ski downhill where you are in control. If you can't negotiate the turns or the hill, take off your skis and walk down the edge of the trail.
- When you fall and make a big hole, fill it in with loose snow.
- Don't take your dogs skiing. Not only do they damage the trails, they chase wildlife and are likely to get hurt by an unsuspecting downhill skier.
- If you are pulling a sled, keep it off well-established tracks or machine-set tracks so you don't obliterate the trail.

Equipment Rental

Cross-country ski rentals are available at the following locations. If you plan to rent equipment from any of these establishments, call to ensure the equipment is available.

West Yellowstone Area

Bud Lilly's Trout Shop
P.O. Box 698
39 Madison Ave.
West Yellowstone, MT 59758
(406) 646-7801

Madison River Outfitters
P.O. Box 1106
117 Canyon Street
West Yellowstone, MT 59758
(406) 646-9644

Northern Yellowstone Park

Mammoth Hot Springs Hotel
TW Recreational Services, Inc.
Yellowstone National Park, WY 82190
(307) 344-7311

The Cooke City Bike Shack
Highway 212
Cooke City, MT 59020
(406) 838-2412

Park's Fly Shop
P.O. Box 196
Gardiner, MT 59030
(406) 848-7314

Old Faithful Area

Old Faithful Snow Lodge
TW Recreational Services, Inc.
Yellowstone National Park, WY 82190
(307) 344-7311

Getting to Old Faithful, Canyon and Other Areas Inside the Park

One of the most popular ways of reaching Old Faithful is by snowcoach—a specially-equipped vehicle on tracks. This has many advantages, probably the greatest of which is the ease and comfort of the trip. All of the planning, packing and driving is left to the snowcoach tour guide, allowing you to relax and enjoy the scenery from the comfort of a heated cabin. Snowcoach tour guides provide information on topics including winter ecology, wildlife, history and geology. If your group is large enough, or your pockets deep enough, you can charter a snowcoach and custom-tailor an itinerary.

On the downside, the speed and schedule of a snowcoach tour may not fit your needs. If you want to ski one of the longer Old Faithful ski trails, you may not be able to find a snowcoach tour that will get you to Old Faithful in time to complete your trek and return to your starting point—West Yellowstone, for example—in a single day. In these cases, you have the choice of either staying at the Old Faithful Snow Lodge, or getting to Old Faithful via snowmobile.

Below is information on the most common snowcoach tours.

Snowcoach Routes:
- South Gate to Old Faithful
- West Yellowstone to Old Faithful
- Mammoth Hot Springs to Old Faithful
- Mammoth Hot Springs to Canyon
- Old Faithful to Canyon
- West Yellowstone to Canyon

Snowcoach Operators:

Flagg Ranch
Box 187, Highway 187
Moran, WY 83013
(307) 733-8761
(800) 443-2311

Moonlight Enterprises
P.O. Box 612
West Yellowstone, MT 59758
(406) 646-7276

TW Recreational Services, Inc.
Yellowstone National Park, WY 82190
(307) 344-7311

Yellowstone Expeditions
P.O. Box 865
511 Gibbon Ave.
West Yellowstone, MT 59758
(406) 646-9333

Yellowstone Alpen Guides Co.
P.O. Box 518
117 Canyon St.
West Yellowstone, MT 59758
(406) 646-9591

Yellowstone Tour and Travel
211 Yellowstone Ave.
West Yellowstone, MT 59758
(406) 646-9310

For the more adventurous, snowmobiles are an alternative for getting into the park. Though it certainly involves more planning and preparation than boarding a snowcoach, it has its advantages. Snowmobiles allow you great freedom in scheduling. You make the decision of when to leave, where you'll stop along the way, and when you'll return.* You can schedule your trip to get an early jump on the other visitors, maybe try some daybreak photography or moonlight skiing, or just allow some extra time for that long ski jaunt. Besides being flexible, a snowmobile trip through the park can be exhilarating.

On the downside, snowmobiling requires lots of effort, both in planning the trip and physical exertion. You will not be able to plop yourself on the snowmobile seat following your ski trip and snooze all the way back to West Yellowstone. There also is a degree of risk in snowmobiling. Though uncommon, you may have a mechanical breakdown, an accident or an unfriendly encounter with a buffalo, or you may risk frostbite or worse if you don't dress properly. In addition, you will have to have a snowmobile sled for getting your skis in and out of the park. Sleds are available at most rental shops.

West Yellowstone is referred to as the "Snowmobile Capital of the World," for good reason. Snowmobile rental establishments abound, so much so that an accurate listing of them is not possible here. Rental snowmobiles are nearly always in ample supply at West Yellowstone; the local telephone directory will provide you with an up-to-date list.

In Gardiner, Montana, snowmobiles may be rented from the Best Western by Mammoth Hot Springs, P.O. Box 646, Gardiner, MT 59030. The telephone number is 1-406-828-9080.

---

* Rented snowmobiles offer somewhat less flexibility since most rental shops keep hours of 8 a.m. - 5 p.m.

Mammoth Hot Springs Ski Trails
General Overview

An 1880s winter visitor poses with his winter gear. (Photo by F. Jay Haynes, courtesy of the Wyoming State Museum.)

Mammoth Hot Springs offers six ski trails from 1.5 to 6 miles long. The terrain often is more challenging than other ski areas in the park. But temperatures tend to be milder. Annual snowfall averages 80 inches.

You will have to use the snowcoach to reach some of the trails. Tickets can be purchased at the front desk of the Mammoth Motor Inn. As this book went to press, round-trip snowcoach shuttle fees to the Bunsen Peak and Indian Creek trailheads were $7. West Yellowstone businesses also offer snowcoach service, though the distance is such that it is unlikely you can ski the Mammoth area and make it back to West Yellowstone in a day. (Snowcoach services are listed in the front section of this book.)

Free bus shuttle service is offered from Mammoth Motor Inn to the Upper Terrace parking lot.

Ski trails are farther from civilization in northern Yellowstone Park. Bring a day pack, snacks, water, warm clothes and a space blanket or similar emergency gear. (See the section in the front of the book on winter safety.) Because many of the trails in the northern portion of the park are longer or are accessible only by shuttle or by driving winter roads, you are going to spend more of the day getting there and less of it skiing.

During the winter, Mammoth Hot Springs can be reached by automobile only from Gardiner, Montana. Follow U.S. Highway 89 through Gardiner, to a 'T.' A sign will point you toward the entrance to Yellowstone National Park. Proceed along this road to Mammoth Hot Springs, the visitor center and other park facilities, 5 miles south of Gardiner.

Park's Fly Shop, in nearby Gardiner, Montana, rents ski equipment and sells U.S. Geological Survey topographic maps. Skis can also be rented at the Bear Den rental shop in Mammoth Hot Springs. We strongly suggest you check at the Albright Visitor Center in Mammoth Hot Springs for the latest information on the trails you want to ski. The Bunsen Peak Trail, for example, can be treacherous if icy, but is much more manageable with new snow.

Indian Creek, Bighorn Loop, Sheepeater Trails

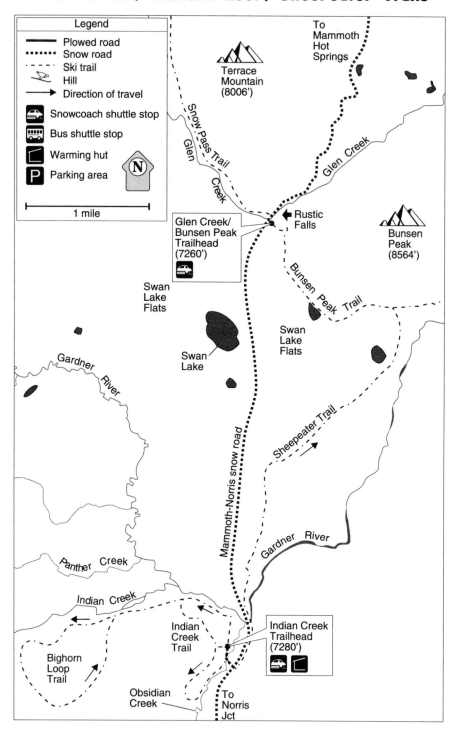

Legend
- —— Plowed road
- ····· Snow road
- – · – Ski trail
- Hill
- → Direction of travel
- Snowcoach shuttle stop
- Bus shuttle stop
- Warming hut
- P Parking area

N

1 mile

Terrace Mountain (8006')

To Mammoth Hot Springs

Snow Pass Trail

Glen Creek

Glen Creek

Rustic Falls

Bunsen Peak (8564')

Glen Creek/ Bunsen Peak Trailhead (7260')

Bunsen Peak Trail

Swan Lake Flats

Swan Lake Flats

Swan Lake

Gardner River

Sheepeater Trail

Mammoth-Norris snow road

Gardner River

Panther Creek

Indian Creek

Indian Creek Trail

Indian Creek Trailhead (7280')

Bighorn Loop Trail

Obsidian Creek

To Norris Jct

Upper Terrace, Snow Pass, Bunsen Peak Trails

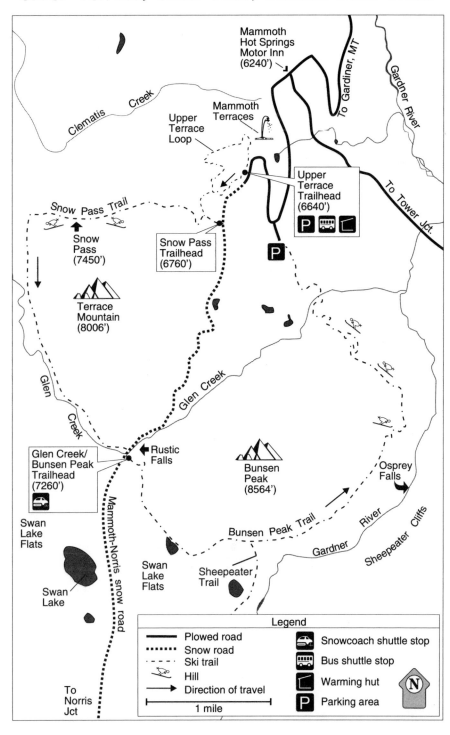

Mammoth
Hot Springs
Motor Inn
(6240')

To Gardiner, MT

Gardner River

Clematis Creek

Upper
Terrace
Loop

Mammoth
Terraces

Upper
Terrace
Trailhead
(6640')

P 🚌 ⬛

To Tower Jct.

Snow Pass Trail

Snow
Pass
(7450')

Snow Pass
Trailhead
(6760')

P

Terrace
Mountain
(8006')

Glen Creek

Glen
Creek

Glen Creek/
Bunsen Peak
Trailhead
(7260')

Rustic
Falls

Bunsen
Peak
(8564')

Osprey
Falls

Swan
Lake
Flats

Mammoth-Norris snow road

Swan
Lake
Flats

Sheepeater
Trail

Bunsen Peak Trail

River

Gardner

Sheepeater Cliffs

Swan
Lake

Legend

—— Plowed road	🚗	Snowcoach shuttle stop
···· Snow road	🚌	Bus shuttle stop
- - - Ski trail	⬛	Warming hut
Hill	P	Parking area
→ Direction of travel	🅝	
⊢ 1 mile ⊣		

To
Norris
Jct

Difficulty:	Easy	

Difficulty: Easy

Length: 2 miles

Grooming: Packed early in the season by snowshoes and tracked by skis at least weekly.

Fee: No fee is charged for skiing, but a general entrance fee is required for Yellowstone National Park.

Overview: This trail makes a 2-mile loop that takes the skier along Indian Creek and Obsidian Creek. Terrain is gentle to moderately rolling.

Location: The trail begins and ends at the Indian Creek Warming Hut, which you reach by snowcoach.

Description: Take the snowcoach from Mammoth Motor Inn to the trailhead at the Indian Creek Warming Hut. (See the front desk at the inn to arrange for a ride; the chapter overview gives current fees.)

The Indian Creek Trail takes off to the right, following the campground road to the north, toward Indian Creek. The trail continues in this direction for approximately 0.25 mile, across level ground, paralleling Obsidian Creek on the right. This stretch of trail is within sight of the Mammoth-Norris snow road on the opposite side of Obsidian Creek.

As the trail nears Indian Creek, it turns sharply to the left and enters the Indian Creek campground. The terrain rolls gently, the forest is semi-open lodgepole pine.

Upon entering Indian Creek campground, the trail veers right (north) to the banks of Indian Creek. For approximately 0.25 mile the trail parallels Indian Creek, heading upriver through gentle terrain.

At this point the trail veers left, away from the creek, into a mature lodgepole pine forest. The trail circles around behind the Indian Creek Campground, crossing gentle terrain. A junction with the Bighorn Loop will be passed on your right. For the more adventurous, a 0.5 mile ski up the Bighorn Loop will bring you to open country, with excellent views of the Gallatin Mountains to the north, across the Indian Creek meadows.

After passing the Bighorn Loop junction, the Indian Creek Trail continues across gentle terrain through dense lodgepole pine forest, mostly burned. In roughly 0.75 mile, the trail reaches its most distant point and turns sharply left, down gentle terrain to the banks of Obsidian Creek. Midway along this stretch a trail branches off to your left and returns directly to the Indian Creek warming hut.

Skiers can see distant timbered ridges up the open valley of Obsidian Creek. From here the trail follows Obsidian Creek downstream to the Indian Creek Warming Hut, 0.5 mile away. Along this stretch the trail follows the edge of a mature lodgepole pine forest across level terrain. The Mammoth-Norris snow road is visible across Obsidian Creek.

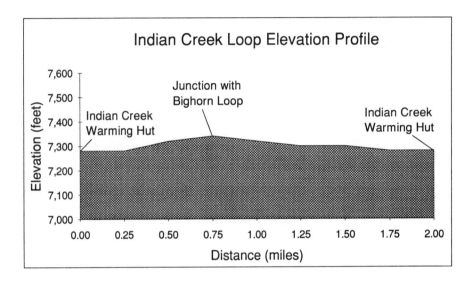

Additional Information: Call the National Park Service at 307-344-2109 (visitor information), or 307-344-7381 (central switchboard). Or write P.O. Box 168, Yellowstone National Park, Wyoming, 82190.

This trail is covered by the U.S. Geological Survey topographical map: Mammoth Quadrangle, WY, 7.5 minute series.

Easy

Difficulty:	Easy
Length:	5 miles
Grooming:	Packed early in the season by snowshoes and tracked by skis at least weekly. But may be obscured by wind-blown snow.
Fee:	No fee is charged for skiing, but a general entrance fee is required for Yellowstone National Park.
Overview:	This trail runs from the Indian Creek Warming Hut through timber to the Bunsen Peak Trail. The terrain is relatively level. Much of the trail winds through live and fire-stripped trees. It provides views of Bunsen Peak and the Gallatin Range. This trail has variety for the skier who has tried everything else in the neighborhood, and it is easy skiing. It does not offer the same spectacular views that other trails provide.
Location:	The trail begins approximately 7 miles south of Mammoth Hot Springs, at the Indian Creek Warming Hut, which you reach by snowcoach. The trail ends at the intersection of the snow road and the Bunsen Peak Trail just south of Rustic Falls at the Glen Creek/Bunsen Peak trailhead. You may want to make arrangements for the snowcoach to pick you up at the trailhead.

Description: Take the snowcoach from Mammoth Motor Inn to the Indian Creek Warming Hut. (Make ride arrangements at the front desk of the inn; the chapter overview gives current fees.)

Ski to the Mammoth-Norris snow road. Turn left and follow the road for 0.5 mile to the Sheepeater Cliffs Picnic Area road. Watch for snowmobiles and snowcoaches along the road.

Veer right slightly, just after the Sheepeater picnic grounds sign, go into the trees and start up a hill. Continue across mostly level terrain through a mixture of live and fire-stripped trees.

The trail follows the east side of Swan Lake Flats, which slowly become visible through the trees. Continue skiing north-northeast for almost 2 miles. As Bunsen Peak comes into view through the trees, the trail veers north.

Watch for rectangular metal orange markers intermittently attached to trees. Orange rods plunged into the snow mark the trail through the meadows. If you lose the trail, aim slightly west (to the left of) Bunsen Peak. The trail weaves down through trees to the Bunsen Peak Trail.

Once you intersect the Bunsen Peak Trail, turn left. Although the Bunsen Peak Trail goes both directions, you will add 4 difficult, downhill miles to your journey if you turn right. (See the Bunsen Peak Trail description for more information.)

For the next 1.8 miles, ski west, then northwest, on mostly level terrain. The trail soon leaves the trees. Swan Lake Flats roll open to the south and the peaks of the Gallatin Range command the horizon to the west. Burned trees skirt much of the bottom of the ridge to the north.

The trail intersects the Mammoth-Norris snow road, just above Rustic Falls at the Glen Creek/Bunsen Peak trailhead. If you have arranged for a snowcoach, you can meet it across the road. If you are skiing back to the Upper Terrace parking lot—another 2.6 miles—turn right. You may have to take off your skis occasionally where woodchips have been laid across bare spots to accommodate snowmobile traffic. You will also have to deal with snowmobiles and snowcoaches along the way.

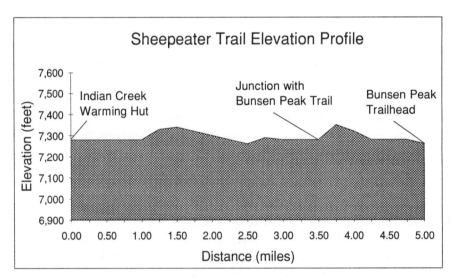

Additional Information: Call the National Park Service at 307-344-2109 (visitor information), or 307-344-7381 (central switchboard). Or write P.O. Box 168, Yellowstone National Park, Wyoming, 82190.

This trail is covered by the U.S. Geological Survey topographical map: Mammoth Quadrangle, WY, 7.5 minute series.

Difficulty:	Moderate

Moderate

Length: 5 miles

Grooming: Packed early in the season by snowshoes and tracked by skis at least weekly.

Fee: No fee is charged for skiing, but a general entrance fee is required for Yellowstone National Park.

Overview: This trail makes a 5-mile loop that takes the skier along Indian Creek through open meadows with exceptional views of the Gallatin Mountains. Terrain is gentle to moderately rolling. Waterfowl are often seen on Indian Creek.

Location: The trail begins and ends at the Indian Creek Warming Hut, on the Mammoth-Norris snow road. You reach the trailhead by snowcoach.

Description: Take the snowcoach from Mammoth Motor Inn to the trailhead at the Indian Creek Warming Hut. (Make arrangements at the front desk of the inn; the chapter overview gives current fees.)

From the hut, the Bighorn Loop ski trail goes right, following the campground road north, toward Indian Creek. The trail continues in this direction for approximately 0.25 mile across level ground, paralleling Obsidian Creek to the right. Along this stretch the trail is within sight of the Mammoth-Norris snow road on the opposite side of Obsidian Creek.

As the trail nears Indian Creek, it turns sharply to the left and enters the Indian Creek campground. The terrain rolls gently, the forest is semi-open lodgepole pine.

Upon entering Indian Creek campground, the trail veers right (north) to the banks of Indian Creek. For approximately 0.25 mile the trail parallels Indian Creek, headed upriver through gentle terrain.

At this point the trail veers left, away from the creek, into a mature lodgepole pine forest. The trail begins to circle around behind the Indian Creek Campground, crossing gentle terrain. You soon encounter a trail junction. The Bighorn Loop turns right, while the Indian Creek Trail continues straight. For approximately 0.5 mile the trail parallels Indian Creek, headed upriver on a roller-coaster trail through burned forest.

At this point the Bighorn Loop trail breaks into the open, with excellent views of the Gallatin Mountains to the north, across the Indian Creek meadows. The trail continues upriver across level terrain, following the edge of a burned forest. As you ski, a panorama of mountains unfolds to the north and west, including Bunsen Peak to the northeast, Quadrant Mountain to the northwest and Antler Peak to the west.

After continuing through the Indian Creek drainage for approximately 0.5 mile, the trail forks. The right branch of the fork is the outward-bound leg of the Bighorn Loop and the left fork is the return leg of the loop. Stay on the right fork of the trail, which continues to parallel Indian Creek across level terrain.

After roughly 0.5 mile, you climb a moderate incline as Indian Creek veers off to your right, out of sight. The trail has reached its farthest point and begins to loop back. It turns to the left and climbs across a low, open hillside to an open knoll. The views are excellent to the north and west.

From here the Bighorn Loop veers left again and begins its return leg. The trail crosses several short, steep hills, then follows a gentle drainage downhill to the loop junction. The forest through this stretch is primarily mature, burned lodgepole pine.

From the loop junction, the skier returns to the Indian Creek Warming Hut by retracing tracks from the outbound journey. For variety, the skier may opt to return to the warming hut via the Indian Creek Ski Trail, which joins the Bighorn Loop Ski Trail near the campground. Look elsewhere in this guide for a description of the Indian Creek Ski Trail.

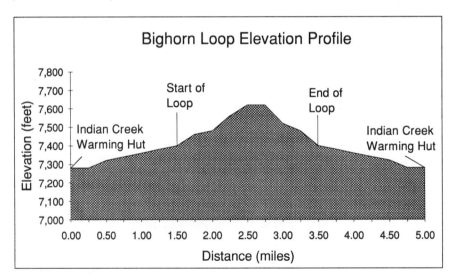

Additional Information: Call the National Park Service at 307-344-2109 (visitor information), or 307-344-7381 (central switchboard). Or write P.O. Box 168, Yellowstone National Park, Wyoming, 82190.

This trail is covered by the U.S. Geological Survey topographical map: Mammoth Quadrangle, WY, 7.5 minute series.

Difficulty:	Moderate

Moderate

Length:	1.5 miles

Grooming: Machine-groomed weekly for track and skate skiing.

Fee: No fee is charged for skiing, but a general entrance fee is required for Yellowstone National Park.

Overview: This is some of the most accessible skiing in northern Yellowstone National Park. This loop follows the Upper Terrace Road around the thermal features just south of the inn at Mammoth Hot Springs. Snow here is often not as deep as other places in the park. The trail offers glimpses of wintering deer and elk and spectacular views of the limestone Mammoth Terraces, the accumulation of eons of mineral deposits laid down by Mammoth Hot Springs. We recommend skiing this trail early in the day, when the trees are still covered with frost.

Location: The loop begins at the Upper Terrace parking lot, about 2 miles from Mammoth Hot Springs and about 7 miles from Gardiner, Montana. Drive or take the free shuttle bus south from Mammoth Hot Springs toward the Mammoth-Norris snow road. Park in the Upper Terrace Loop parking lot on your right.

Description: You may ski this trail in either direction. We've described it as a clockwise loop, which gets the uphill portion out of the way immediately. But skiing counterclockwise has its benefits—you'll reach the thermal features faster, and be rewarded with a fast downhill ski at the end.

Pick up the ski trail at the north end of the parking lot and head west into the trees. Turn left almost immediately and begin climbing through trees. Watch for skiers coming downhill.

The trail climbs about 200 feet in the first 0.75 mile. About 0.5 mile along, the first thermal feature—Angel Terrace—appears through the trees to your right. The trail continues to curve and climb.

If you want to catch the Snow Pass Trail, begin looking for orange trail markers nailed to trees on your left at the top of the hill before you reach White Elephant Back Terrace. The Snow Pass access goes south, on your left through the trees, and joins the Snow Pass Trail in a short distance. The terrace is next. It is a long mound, built by mineral-laden water, and is said to resemble marching elephants.

The view of the Absaroka-Beartooth Range to the north is magnificent on a clear day. The Gardner River Canyon is off to the east.

The trail winds downward in tight S-curves from White Elephant Back Terrace and levels briefly. After a short, steep climb, the trail gently meanders down to the bright splendor of Orange Spring Mound.

The grade becomes steeper from here, bringing the skier rapidly to the stark tree skeletons at New Highland Spring. This relatively young thermal feature has been masking the landscape with travertine for only about 40 years.

The trail continues down, soon making a sharp left turn followed by a long descent that takes you out on a bench. From here you can see the Lower Terraces that spill toward Mammoth Hot Springs. On a clear day, the view is unmatched.

From here the trail is a continuous right-hand curve, downhill at first and then going up. The trail from the parking lot soon intersects the Upper Terrace Loop. Go left to return to your vehicle or the shuttle bus.

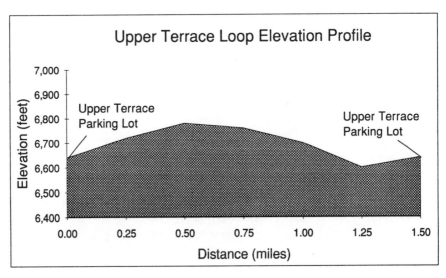

Additional Information: Call the National Park Service at 307-344-2109 (visitor information), or 307-344-7381 (central switchboard). Or write P.O. Box 168, Yellowstone National Park, Wyoming, 82190.

This trail is covered by the U.S. Geological Survey topographical map: Mammoth Quadrangle, WY, 7.5 minute series.

Difficulty:	Difficult (Extreme if the trail is icy and you ski opposite the direction suggested here. Check conditions at the Albright Visitor Center in Mammoth Hot Springs.)

Difficult

Length: 4.2 miles if you use the snowcoach to return. Skiing back to the Upper Terrace parking lot along the Mammoth-Norris snow road, which is frequented by snowmobiles, adds 2.6 miles.

Grooming: Packed early in the season by snowshoes and tracked by skis at least weekly. But may be obscured by wind-blown snow.

Fee: No fee is charged for skiing, but a general entrance fee is required for Yellowstone National Park.

Overview: This loop includes a steep climb around the north side of Terrace Mountain to a fairly level valley, then winds along the edge of Swan Lake Flats. If you own climbing skins, you'll want them for skiing this trail in the traditional direction. There is a challenging hill, with a 700-foot climb in 1.5 miles. (It is an exhilarating but difficult trip if you ski the trail in reverse direction from Rustic Falls back toward the Upper Terrace area.) The rest of the journey is a pleasant ski on mostly level terrain.

Location: The trail can be reached from three locations. You can park at the Upper Terrace Loop and ski that trail to White Elephant Back Terrace. Veer left on a trail marked by orange rectangles nailed to the trees to reach the Snow Pass trail in about 0.25 mile. The trail also can be reached from the Mammoth-Norris snow road, about 0.3 mile south of the Upper Terrace parking area. You will have to leave your vehicle or the free shuttle bus at the parking lot and ski up the road. Or, to ski the trail in its difficult reverse direction, catch a snowcoach to the Glen Creek/Bunsen Peak trailhead near Rustic Falls by making arrangements at the front desk of the Mammoth Motor Inn. (See the chapter overview for current fees.) That same shuttle will fetch you from the Glen Creek/Bunsen Peak trailhead if you end your trip there.

Description: The trail begins its 700-foot climb westward from the snow road through dense trees. Depending on snow depth, you may soon encounter a summer hiking trail registry. Go straight to get to Snow Pass.

The trail uphill becomes steeper, with some sharp turns, and occasionally levels out briefly in more open areas. Mount Everts and Bunsen Peak are visible behind you from time to time. The steady climb continues to the top of the pass. It is laborious and requires almost continuous herringbone without climbing skins. It is hard to overstate the exertion required by all but experienced skiers.

The trail meets a powerline and follows it over the top of Snow Pass. Since the timber is fairly dense, the views are limited. After descending into the Glen Creek drainage from Snow Pass, you may see markers for two unmaintained trails, one leading up the Glen Creek Drainage, the other crossing Glen Creek. These trails are summer hiking trails and are not maintained for skiing. Do not attempt these trails without consulting a ranger.

From here, orange snowpoles mark the trail's course across open meadows. The terrain is level, following an old wagon road around the slopes at the base of Terrace Mountain. As it leaves the valley, the trail picks up the northern edge of Swan Lake Flats and the Gallatin Mountains come into view. The open slopes to your left offer some great telemarking opportunities, if you have the energy after climbing the pass.

The trail gradually turns east. It meets the Mammoth-Norris snow road about 0.75 mile later at the Glen Creek/Bunsen Peak trailhead. Turn left if you plan to ski the 2.6 miles back to the Upper Terrace parking lot. Remember snowmobiles also use this road. You can make prior arrangements at the Mammoth Motor Inn to catch the snowcoach back to the Upper Terrace parking lot from the Glen Creek/Bunsen Peak trailhead.

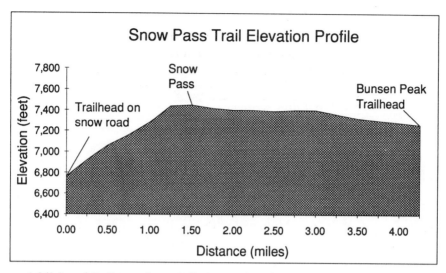

Snow Pass Trail Elevation Profile

Additional Information: Call the National Park Service at 307-344-2109 (visitor information), or 307-344-7381 (central switchboard). Or write P.O. Box 168, Yellowstone National Park, Wyoming, 82190.

This trail is covered by the U.S. Geological Survey topographical map: Mammoth Quadrangle, WY, 7.5 minute series.

28

Difficult

Difficulty: Difficult. The first 3 miles are easy; much of the rest of the trail is steep downhill with hairpin turns that are treacherous if icy. Check with rangers at the Albright Visitor Center in Mammoth Hot Springs before skiing this trail.

Length: 6 miles

Grooming: Machine groomed for track skiing weekly. Tracks occasionally obscured by wind-blown snow.

Fee: No fee is charged for skiing, but a general entrance fee is required for Yellowstone National Park.

Overview: This trail takes you from the Mammoth-Norris snow road along the edge of Swan Lake Flats and around the south and east sides of Bunsen Peak. The first half of the trail is easy but the second half includes extremely challenging hairpin turns that drop 960 feet in 2 miles. The trail loops back to a parking area about 1.5 miles south of Mammoth Hot Springs. **WARNING:** There's absolutely no room for error on the curves, which can be icy. Check on trail conditions at the Albright Visitor Center in Mammoth Hot Springs before skiing here. We recommend only skiers confident of their turning ability try this portion of the trail, which is great fun under the right conditions. The first half of the trail includes beautiful views of the Gallatin Mountains, Swan Lake Flats, and Gardner River Canyon. You can ski in 3 miles, turn around and return to the Mammoth-Norris snow road, for 6 miles of fairly easy skiing. You can also pick up the Sheepeater Trail, about 1.8 miles east of where the Bunsen Peak Trail leaves the Mammoth-Norris road.

Location: The trail begins at the Glen Creek/Bunsen Peak trailhead just above Rustic Falls, on the Mammoth-Norris snow road, about 5 miles from Mammoth Hot Springs. You can take a snowcoach from the inn to the starting point. If you are not going to ski the entire loop, you may want to make arrangements for the snowcoach to pick you up at the drop-off. Make all arrangements ahead of time at the front desk of the Mammoth Motor Inn. (See the chapter overview for current fees.)

Description: The trail heads east across a meadow from the Mammoth-Norris snow road, soon turning southeast and following the bottom of a ridge at the base of Bunsen Peak. Burned trees—remnants of the fires of 1988 —are found along much of this ridge. The impressive view south across Swan Lake Flats includes Quadrant Mountain (elev. 10,261 feet) and Bannock Peak (elev. 10,323 feet), both part of the Gallatin Mountain Range.

From Swan Lake Flats, the trail enters a forest where many of the trees are blackened by fire. The trail starts to rise gently as it draws closer to the south side of Bunsen Peak. At 1.8 miles, a junction with the Sheepeater Trail is encountered. Turn right onto Sheepeater Trail if you plan this side trip of 5 miles. Be sure you've arranged for a snowcoach pick-up because the Sheepeater Trail takes you to the Indian Creek Warming Hut, a fair distance from Mammoth Hot Springs.

The trail levels out in a stand of stark, fire-stripped trees. The lower slopes of Bunsen Peak provide inviting telemark possibilities.

The trail drops to the right, in gentle S-curves through the trees, levels slightly and drops again. The Sheepeater Cliffs—named for the Sheepeater Indians who once frequented the area—come into view. Here you should begin to see Sheepeater Canyon, carved by the feisty Gardner River.

The trees thin on the left, affording a better view of Bunsen Peak (elev. 8,564 feet). The trail begins to climb, veering left (north) and pulling away from the canyon. It levels again as an aspen grove appears to your right and then begins a slight descent, winding into a burned-out stand of trees. A road sign here says "Road Narrows." Plan to turn around here unless you are prepared for the upcoming difficult downhill section.

From here, the trail winds gently through the trees for a short distance. Watch for a "Steep Grade" road sign indicating the start of your plunge towards Glen Creek. Be prepared for a sharp right turn, followed immediately by a sharp left turn and another sharp right. This pattern continues for most of the next 2 miles.

Do not venture through the trees off the established trail to the canyon edge. Snow cornices on the edge collapse easily, and that would send you into Sheepeater Canyon.

The turns become sharper. Because of the tight turns and nearby trees, you have little room for error. There are no good snowdrifts to crash into if you lose control. In a few places, where the trees are less dense, the edge of the trail is dangerously close to the canyon.

About 0.5 mile from where the descent begins, the trail levels and you can stop and look back at Osprey Falls. The trail climbs for 0.2 mile, levels and then begins to drop again. The buildings at Mammoth Hot Springs come into view to the north and the Absaroka Range looms to the east.

After a long straight stretch—with trees separating you from the nearby precipice—curves begin again. Though the curves are more gentle than before, this winding downhill descent lasts about 0.4 mile and leads to an extremely sharp right turn. This is followed by several tight turns as the trail races down through dense trees.

About 0.8 mile later the trail bottoms out at Glen Creek. After crossing Glen Creek, which is usually obscured by snow, the trail immediately starts a short, steep climb, then levels out and crosses an open meadow. In 0.5 mile the trail ends at a plowed road near a National Park Service housing area. Follow this road right for approximately 0.25 mile to the main road, where you can flag down a shuttle van. If you turn left at the main road, you can reach the Upper Terrace Parking area about 1 mile away and it is served by a shuttle. A right turn will take you to Mammoth Hot Springs, about 1.5 miles away.

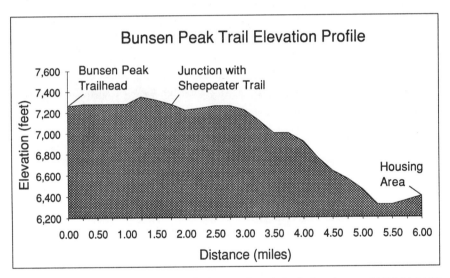

Additional Information: Call the National Park Service at 307-344-2109 (visitor information), or 307-344-7381 (central switchboard). Or write P.O. Box 168, Yellowstone National Park, Wyoming, 82190.

This trail is covered by the U.S. Geological Survey topographical map: Mammoth Quadrangle, WY, 7.5 minute series.

Tower Junction Ski Trails
General Overview

On the right day, elk are visible from many Yellowstone Trails. (Photo by Ken Olsen.)

From the Petrified Tree to vistas of the Blacktail Plateau, the Tower area offers spectacular skiing. Getting here requires driving 23 miles across the only road kept open year-round in Yellowstone National Park. Shuttle bus service is available to three of the four trailheads, for a fee.

If you're driving, go south from Gardiner, Montana, to Mammoth Hot Springs. Turn left at a clearly marked junction, following the road to Tower Junction, about 18 miles away. If you are planning to ski either the Blacktail Plateau Trail or the Lost Lake Trail, you will not go all of the way to Tower Junction. Check the individual trail descriptions.

The shuttle bus offers drops at the beginning of the Blacktail Plateau Trail, near the Lost Lake Trail and near the Tower Falls Trail. Make arrangements in advance at the Mammoth Motor Inn, and if you miss your return ride, notify the desk when you get back lest they mount a full-scale search. As this book went to press, round-trip bus shuttle fees to Tower Junction ski trails were $8.60 for adults, $4.30 for children.

Take extra precautions when skiing this far from civilization. Always pack an extra ski tip, be prepared for blizzards and surprises (like your car not starting when you return from the ski trail). Take snacks and water along. See the section on winter safety at the front of the book for a list of suggested gear.

Coyote and elk droppings can be problematic. If you get them on your skis, the droppings stick to the wax and kill your glide. Also avoid the buffalo that frequent this area.

Many people ski both ways on Tower area trails, so be alert for downhill skiers. Trail courtesy calls for the uphill skier to yield the tracks to the downhill skier. Uphill skiers should not stop in the middle of the track to visit, eat or get a drink of water, especially on blind curves. Avoid skiing more than two abreast.

If you need to call for help, there are telephones at the Tower Falls Store and east of the service station at Tower Junction. Both of these establishments are closed during the winter season.

Lost Lake, Tower Falls, Chittenden Loop Trails

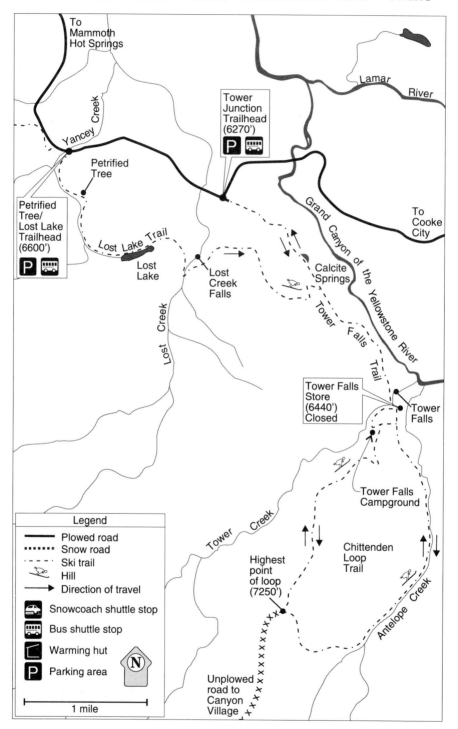

To Mammoth Hot Springs

Yancey Creek

Yancey

Lamar River

Tower Junction Trailhead (6270')

P 🚌

Petrified Tree

Petrified Tree/ Lost Lake Trailhead (6600')

P 🚌

Lost Lake Trail

Lost Lake

Lost Creek Falls

Lost Creek

To Cooke City

Grand Canyon of the Yellowstone River

Calcite Springs

Tower Falls Trail

Tower Falls Store (6440') Closed

Tower Falls

Tower Falls Campground

Tower Creek

Highest point of loop (7250')

Chittenden Loop Trail

Antelope Creek

Unplowed road to Canyon Village

Legend

— Plowed road
••••••• Snow road
- - - Ski trail
🎿 Hill
→ Direction of travel
🚐 Snowcoach shuttle stop
🚌 Bus shuttle stop
🏠 Warming hut
P Parking area

N

1 mile

34

Blacktail Plateau Trail

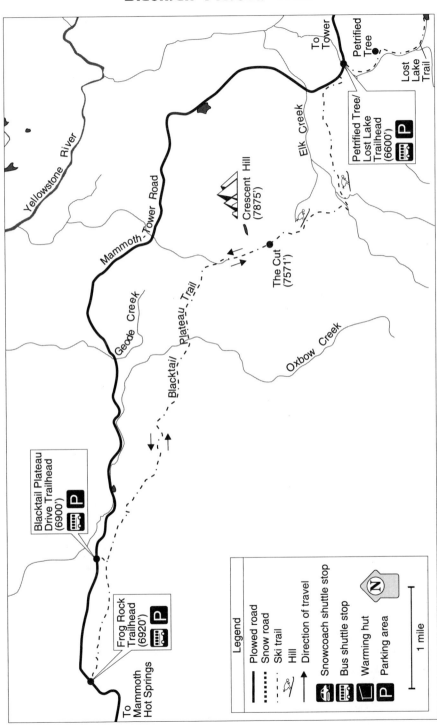

Tower Falls

Difficulty:	Moderate. An easy 3-mile round trip can be made by skiing to the Calcite Springs overlook and back.

Moderate

Length: 5 miles round trip.

Grooming: Tracks are often machine-set.

Fee: No fee is charged for skiing, but a general entrance fee is required for Yellowstone National Park.

Overview: This trail follows the unplowed Tower-Canyon road for 2.5 miles. You follow the same path out and back. This is not a loop like most Yellowstone ski trails. It is perfect for people who want a short but hearty climb, great views of the Grand Canyon of the Yellowstone River and the chance to see Bighorn Sheep and other wildlife.

Location: Begins 18 miles east of Mammoth Hot Springs at Tower Junction. The Mammoth-Cooke City highway is open to automobile traffic year-round. You can get to the Tower Falls ski trail by automobile or by shuttle bus service available from Mammoth Motor Inn. Make arrangements at the inn's front desk. If you miss your pick-up, notify the front desk upon your return to prevent initiation of search and rescue operations. (See chapter overview for current fees.)

Description: The Tower Falls Trail heads east and then south from Tower Junction, following the unplowed Tower-Canyon road. The winding road climbs gradually at first and becomes steeper as you progress along the first mile. Elk, mule deer and buffalo may be on or near the road.

The trail levels out briefly as it approaches Calcite Springs Overlook, on your left about 1.5 miles from the beginning of the trail. The overlook is worth checking out for a splendid view of the Grand Canyon of the Yellowstone River. Bighorn sheep may be visible across the canyon.

The trail continues its ascent briefly. The Grand Canyon of the Yellowstone, rimmed with basalt columns, soon becomes visible from the trail. A hundred yards later, the trail begins to descend. Check for bighorn sheep on the ridge to the east. Your view of the canyon improves and you can see the Yellowstone River.

Avoid skiing too close to the edge at the overlooks. Watch for chunks of basalt, sharp as broken glass, that fall onto the ski track from the cliffs above. Skiing over them will damage your skis.

From here the trail drops slightly, following gentle curves to Tower Falls. Do not attempt to ski down to the base of the falls. (Depending on the time of year, a foot trail to the falls is kept well-packed by visitors.) Check with park service personnel—avalanches fall into the road from steep road cuts here, particularly after heavy snows or when the weather is warm.

Return to your car or the shuttle bus pick-up by retracing the trail that brought you to Tower Falls.

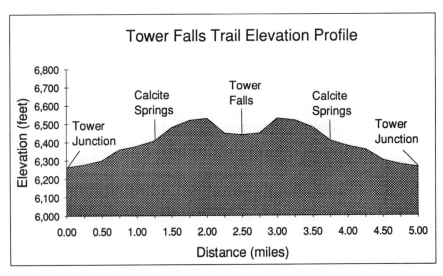

Additional Information: Call the National Park Service at 307-344-2109 (visitor information) or 307-344-7381 (central switchboard). Or write P.O. Box 168, Yellowstone National Park, Wyoming, 82190.

This trail is covered by the U.S. Geological Survey topographical map: Tower Junction Quadrangle, WY, 7.5 minute series.

Moderate

Difficulty:	Moderate, with some difficult sections if hard-packed or icy.
Length:	5 miles
Grooming:	Tracked by skiers.
Fee:	No fee is charged for skiing, but a general entrance fee is required for Yellowstone National Park.
Overview:	This trail offers a great deal of variety in terrain and scenery. The trail takes the skier up the steep-walled drainage of Yancey Creek, past Lost Lake, along precipitous cliffs that overlook Lost Creek Falls, then across varied terrain to Calcite Springs Overlook, and finally, down a portion of the Tower-Canyon road that is maintained exclusively for cross-country skiing during winter.
Location:	The trail begins about 15 miles east of Mammoth Hot Springs, or 1.5 miles west of Tower Junction, on the Mammoth-Tower road. The trailhead is at the Petrified Tree access road pull-out. The trail ends at the parking area just east of Tower Junction.
	The Mammoth-Tower road is open to automobile traffic year-round. You can get to the Lost Lake ski trail by automobile or by shuttle bus service available from Mammoth Motor Inn. Make arrangements at the inn's front desk. If you miss your pick-up, notify the front desk upon your return to prevent initiation of search and rescue operations. (See chapter overview for current fees.)

Description: From the trailhead at the Petrified Tree turnoff, the trail follows the unplowed access road for about 0.4 mile to the Petrified Tree. This portion of the trail climbs gently up the steep-walled drainage of Yancey Creek. The forest is patchy here, some live and some burned trees. The Petrified Tree is on your left.

The Lost Lake ski trail crosses to the far right corner of the Petrified Tree parking area, then drops slightly into the Lost Lake drainage, continuing up this drainage for 0.5 mile to Lost Lake. The drainage along this stretch is narrow, but the bottom is easy skiing with gentle slopes and no trees or brush to impede progress. The surrounding hillsides have mature Douglas-fir, mostly live. The drainage opens up as you near Lost Lake.

The trail follows the left (north) side of the lake. As you ski along Lost Lake, the hillsides flatten. At the end of the lake, a small stream cascades down a narrow canyon. You can see the Absaroka/Beartooth mountain ranges to the northeast, directly over Tower Junction.

The trail veers right after leaving the lake, proceeding through mostly level terrain covered with dense lodgepole pine. You may see a sign (if it's not buried by snow) indicating a junction with a summer hiking trail that leads down to Roosevelt Lodge. The summer hiking trail is not maintained as a ski trail and should not be attempted, because it crosses extremely steep terrain. At this trail junction you are just over 1 mile from the Petrified Tree.

In less than 0.25 mile you come to the narrow canyon of Lost Creek. You skirt this canyon, in the upstream direction, and cross Lost Creek on a small footbridge. After crossing the creek you climb a slope on the opposite side of the creek and ski back in the same direction as which you came. The terrain is gently rolling; the forest is dense, with small lodgepole pine.

As you follow Lost Creek downstream, the creek falls away on your left and is soon several hundred feet below you in a steep-walled canyon. As you ski this stretch, you parallel a bluff on the edge of Pleasant Valley, the valley where Tower Junction lies. The skier is occasionally favored with views of the Absaroka/Beartooth mountain ranges to the north.

Approximately 0.5 mile after leaving Lost Lake you reach the Lost Creek Falls overlook and an excellent view down sheer cliffs to the 120-foot Lost Creek Falls below. **WARNING:** do not ski too close to the canyon edge. Remove your skis anytime you venture out to look at the canyon and be very cautious! Snow cornices present a lethal hazard.

From the Lost Creek Falls overlook the trail climbs gently, continuing to parallel Pleasant Valley. After a short but steep downhill run through dense forest, the trail turns right across an open meadow. At this point you may see a sign (if it's not buried by snow) that indicates a junction with a summer hiking trail that leads down to Roosevelt corrals. This summer hiking trail is not maintained as a ski trail and should not be attempted, because it crosses extremely steep terrain. At this trail junction you are more than 2 miles from the Petrified Tree.

The trail continues across the open meadow, then across rolling terrain with alternating forest and meadows. Mount Washburn and the Lamar Valley are visible on the left. After another 0.5 mile, the trail turns abruptly left on an open hillside. At this point you may see a sign that indicates a summer hiking trail straight ahead to Tower Falls campground. As with the other summer trails encountered, this hiking trail is not maintained for skiing and should not be attempted. Look for a large orange ski-trail marker on your left.

Upon leaving the Tower Falls hiking trail, the Lost Lake ski trail makes a diagonal run down an open, moderately steep hillside. The trail then switchbacks down a steep forested grade for the last 0.25 mile to the Calcite Springs overlook. These curves are hair-raising when hard-packed or icy.

From the Calcite Springs overlook, the skier returns to Tower Junction via a stretch of the Tower-Canyon road that is maintained exclusively for cross-country skiing. This section of the trail offers a wide skiing surface, excellent for practicing one's diagonal stride on the flats and downhill techniques on the moderate downhill sections. Distance from the Calcite Springs Overlook to Tower Junction is 1.5 miles.

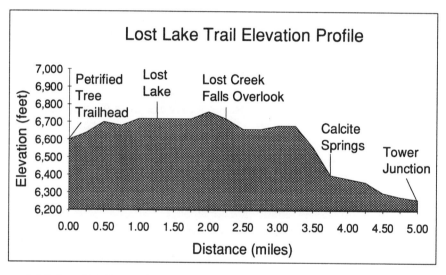

Additional Information: Call the National Park Service at 307-344-2109 (visitor information), or 307-344-7381 (central switchboard). Or write P.O. Box 168, Yellowstone National Park, Wyoming, 82190.

This trail is covered by the U.S. Geological Survey topographical map: Tower Junction Quadrangle, WY, 7.5 minute series.

Difficulty:	Difficult

Difficult

Length: 7 miles one way from the Blacktail Plateau Drive trailhead, or 8 miles one way from the Frog Rock trailhead.

Grooming: Tracked by machine when conditions permit.

Fee: No fee is charged for skiing, but a general entrance fee is required for Yellowstone National Park.

Overview: This trail, which follows an unplowed road, is highly recommended for great views, wildlife and a long downhill stretch on the last half of the trail. **WARNING**: Blacktail Plateau is a heavily used, two-way trail. Watch for skiers coming from the opposite direction, especially on curves and steep hills. Uphill skiers should yield the tracks to downhill skiers. Do not stop in the tracks, particularly on steep hills or where terrain blocks the view. If you snowplow, try not to obliterate the tracks.

Location: This trail starts from two different places. The preferred access is a parking area 8.5 miles west of Mammoth Hot Springs on the Mammoth-Tower road at a place called Frog Rock. There is more parking available here. You can also park about 9.5 miles from Mammoth Hot Springs near a sign that reads "Blacktail Plateau Drive." You will have to spot an automobile at both the beginning and end, turn back along the way, or rely on the shuttle bus, which stops at both ends of the trail. Bus arrangements must be made at the Mammoth Motor Inn in advance. (See chapter overview for current fees.)

Description: From the parking area at Frog Rock, ski west for about 1 mile across gently rolling, open terrain. Here you encounter a junction with the trail originating at the Blacktail Plateau Drive trailhead. This trail junction can sometimes be easily overlooked, depending on the number of skiers using the Blacktail Plateau Drive entrance.

From the junction, the trail climbs up a gentle incline through a mixture of aspen, Douglas-fir and burned relics of the 1988 fires.

In about 0.3 mile, the trail levels out and draws into a broad open meadow.

The views to the north and west open up. Be sure to turn around from time to time and enjoy the mountains on the western horizon. Elk, coyote and deer may move in and out of the trees.

About 0.5 mile later, the trail begins a moderately steep climb through a draw and then emerges into open terrain. A metal gate marks a spur road to the right, which may or may not be visible, depending upon snow depth.

The trail continues to climb steadily for another 0.5 mile. Huge Douglas-fir trees are on your right. The trail levels, enters a draw, and resumes climbing, gently and then more steeply.

Within about 0.2 mile, you emerge from the draw. The view behind you is especially spectacular. Soon a group of trees on the ridge to the south shows evidence of the fires of 1988.

Alternating between level stretches and inclines, the trail winds on for about another 0.3 mile. The trail begins to hug Crescent Hill, on your left, and passes through an area called The Cut, where the trail is flanked on both sides by steep slopes that can avalanche.

From here to the end, skiing is sheer downhill joy on switchbacks that drop into stretches of dense forest, some of it burned in 1988. When the trail is hard-packed, crusty or icy, you may want to turn back at The Cut.

While most of the curves are only moderately difficult, be alert. Not long after you leave The Cut there is a fairly tight turn to the left, followed by a long descent. Beginning skiers may want to proceed slowly.

A ridge, with skeletons of fire-killed trees, soon weaves its way into the picture from your right. Turns here are sharper. The descent steepens.

The switchbacks draw you into a stark, black-and-white stand of burned trees. Prepare for an extremely sharp left turn. Steep turns continue through burned trees.

Then the straight stretches become longer, though the trees remain dense. The grade eases and the trees thin momentarily, with live trees beginning to outnumber dead ones.

The Mammoth-Tower road will briefly pop into view on your left. The trail levels, climbs slightly through a meadow, curves to the left and soon intersects a metal gate, possibly buried by snow. The Mammoth-Tower road is just beyond. A parking area and shuttle bus stop are nearby, to the right. Use caution when skiing along the Mammoth-Tower road. Don't ski on the road or the berm created by snowplows.

From the end of the Blacktail Plateau trail you can also connect to the Lost Lake Ski Trail. To do this, follow a short trail to the right that crosses Yancey Creek on a footbridge and joins the Lost Lake trail midway between the Mammoth-Tower road and the Petrified Tree.

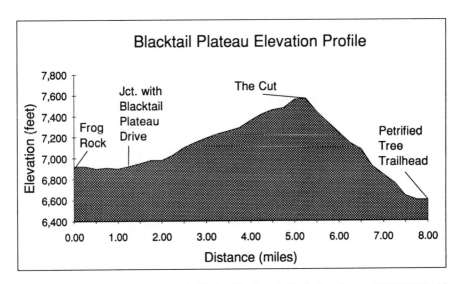

Additional Information: Call the National Park Service at 307-344-2109 (visitor information), or 307-344-7381 (central switchboard). Or write P.O. Box 168, Yellowstone National Park, Wyoming, 82190.

This trail is covered by the U.S. Geological Survey topographical maps:
Tower Junction Quadrangle, WY, 7.5 minute series
Blacktail Deer Creek Quadrangle, WY, 7.5 minute series

Difficulty:	Difficult
Length:	10.25 miles round trip from Tower Junction.
Grooming:	Track may be machine-set.
Fee:	No fee is charged for skiing, but a general entrance fee is required for Yellowstone National Park.
Overview:	This trail is a long sustained uphill that provides great exercise, followed by a long sustained downhill that can be lots of fun on fresh snow. Views are scarce, and tend toward open hillsides rather than lofty peaks or expansive vistas. Much of the trail traverses dense lodgepole pine forests, some of them burned by the fires of 1988. The trail follows the Tower-Canyon road and the Chittenden service road for its entire length.
Location:	This trail begins at what in the summertime is the Tower Falls Store parking area. Follow the Tower Falls trail (described previously in this chapter) 2.5 miles to get to this trailhead. The Chittenden Loop is 5.3 miles, but skiing to and from the Tower Falls trailhead adds 5 miles.

Description: Follow the Tower Falls trail (described previously in this chapter) to Tower Falls. From the Tower Falls Store parking area, ski westward toward the Tower Falls Campground. (A sign points to the campground.) The trail climbs steeply and levels out briefly as it loops into the campground.

After a gentle left turn, the trail turns right (south) onto a service road and begins climbing for most of the next 2 miles through dense lodgepole pine.

About 0.5 mile above the campground, the trail winds through a dense pocket of mature Douglas-fir, then rounds a corner to emerge on an open, burnt hillside overlooking the Tower Creek drainage. Stark, rolling hills of burnt forest command the view across Tower Creek. Behind you, catch a glimpse of the yellowish wall of the Grand Canyon of the Yellowstone River.

The trail continues its fairly steep climb, leveling somewhat in about another 0.5 mile. After crossing the open hillside, the trail continues along the service road through a corridor of dense lodgepole pine, some live, some burned.

The trail levels out, climbs, levels out. After approximately 1 mile you come to the unplowed Tower-Canyon road. Bear left for a 3-mile ski back to the Tower Falls area. This portion of the trail is nearly all downhill on machine-groomed trail. It offers great opportunity to practice downhill technique, as well as turning and snowplowing (please step out of the track to practice the latter.) From the Tower Falls area, follow the Tower Falls Trail (described previously in this chapter) another 2.5 miles to the Tower Junction parking lot.

More experienced skiers may want to ski this trail in the opposite direction to enjoy the fast downhill that you otherwise laboriously ski up early on. Another option for strong skiers is skiing past the intersection of the Tower Falls Road and the Chittenden service road for lunch with grand views of the Antelope Creek Valley and Mount Washburn.

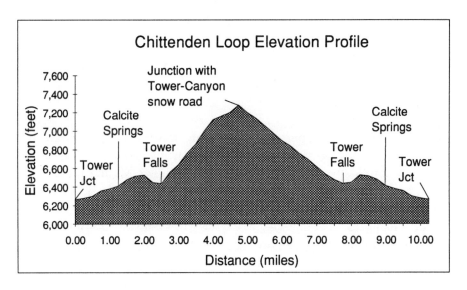

Additional Information: Call the National Park Service at 307-344-2109 (visitor information), or 307-344-7381 (central switchboard). Or write P.O. Box 168, Yellowstone National Park, Wyoming, 82190.

This trail is covered by the U.S. Geological Survey topographical maps:
Tower Junction Quadrangle, WY, 7.5 minute series
Mount Washburn Quadrangle, WY, 7.5 minute series

Northeast Yellowstone Ski Trails
General Overview

The northeastern corner of Yellowstone National Park offers 3 marked ski trails. The longest trail—Pebble Creek—is not groomed, meaning skiers likely face 13 miles of unbroken snow. There are other ski trails close to Cooke City, Montana, just beyond the northeastern entrance to the park.

The northeast corner of Yellowstone National Park has higher elevations and more vertical relief than any other section of the park. This corner of the park sees cold temperatures and heavy snowfalls similar to West Yellowstone.

The ski trails of Northeast Yellowstone can be reached by automobile or shuttle bus, but only with some degree of effort. As this book went to press, shuttle bus service was available from the Mammoth Hot Springs Motor Inn to the Northeast Yellowstone trailheads on Tuesdays and Fridays only. The shuttle service is a day-long tour which leaves at 8:30 a.m. and returns at 5:30 p.m.. Round-trip cost is $45. Inquire at the front desk of the Mammoth Motor Inn concerning current costs and scheduling.

If you choose to drive your own automobile, the Cooke City area is around 60 miles from Mammoth Hot Springs. Please note that in winter, the road is only plowed as far as Cooke City, Montana. The only way out is driving back to Mammoth Hot Springs, up to Gardiner, Montana, and on to Livingston, Montana.

Because we believe these factors mean the general skier is less likely to ski this area, we have covered the area in less depth. We have included maps and elevation profiles, but the trail descriptions are more brief.

We hope this won't discourage the more adventurous who will find spectacular scenery and good telemarking here. Check with the National Park Service for avalanche and snow conditions before venturing far off the established trails.

The Cooke City Bike Shack rents ski equipment.

Northeast Yellowstone Trails

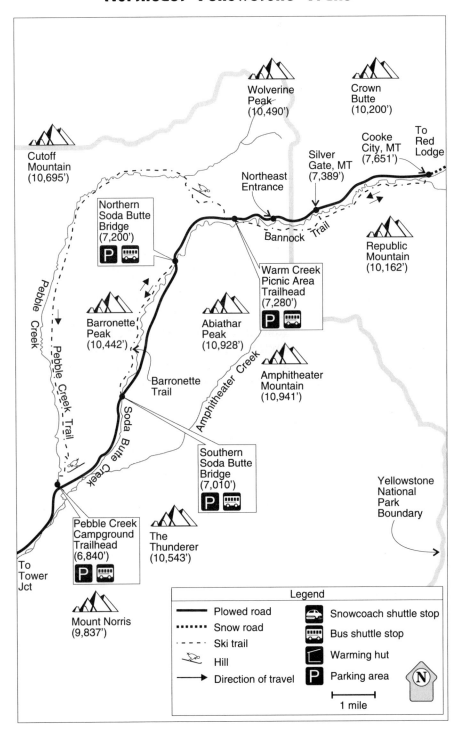

Easy

Difficulty:	Easy
Length:	2 miles one way
Grooming:	Skied after each major snowfall
Fee:	No fee is charged for skiing, but a general entrance fee is required for Yellowstone National Park.
Overview:	A short, easy trail over level terrain. The trail follows the roadbed of the old Cooke City highway from the Warm Creek Picnic Area to Silver Gate, Montana. An additional 3-mile ski along a snowmobile trail will take you to Cooke City, Montana. This trail is not a loop—you will have to ski out and back or spot a car at your destination.
Location:	The trail begins at the Warm Creek Picnic Area 1 mile west of the Northeast Entrance of Yellowstone National Park, 5 miles west of Cooke City, Montana. The only winter access to this trailhead is via Mammoth Hot Springs (see chapter overview). From Gardiner, Montana, drive 5 miles south to Mammoth Hot Springs. Turn left on the Mammoth-Tower road and drive 18 miles to Tower Junction. Turn left and drive about 28 miles to the Warm Creek Picnic Area. The trailhead is about 52 miles from Gardiner.

Description: From the parking area at the Warm Creek Picnic Area the trail crosses Soda Butte Creek, then turns left (east), up the broad valley floor. The trail follows the roadbed of the old Cooke City highway, crossing nearly flat terrain as it travels through a mix of open meadows and forest. Abiathar Peak (10,928'), Amphitheater Mountain (10,652'), and Republic Mountain (10,170') form a wall of mountains to the south.

At roughly 1 mile you leave Yellowstone National Park and enter the North Absaroka Wilderness of the Shoshone National Forest. At 2 miles the trail veers left to leave the wilderness area near Silver Gate, Montana. The trail meets a snowmobile trail on the outskirts of Silver Gate. Turn left to end your ski at Silver Gate, or continue along the snowmobile trail to reach Cooke City in another 3 miles of easy skiing. A relaxing lunch at Cooke City before returning to the trailhead makes for a full day with 10 miles of skiing.

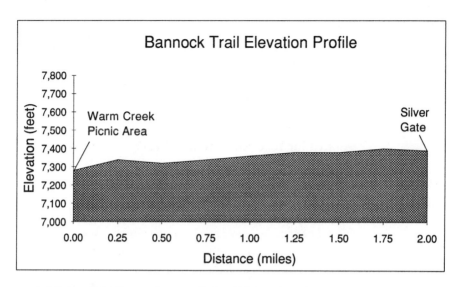

Additional Information: Call the National Park Service at 307-344-2109 (visitor information), or 307-344-7381 (central switchboard). Or write P.O. Box 168, Yellowstone National Park, Wyoming, 82190.

This trail is covered by the U.S. Geological Survey topographical maps:
Cooke City Quadrangle, MT-WY, 7.5 minute series
Cutoff Mountain Quadrangle, MT-WY, 7.5 minute series

Difficulty:	Easy
Length:	3.5 miles one way
Grooming:	Skied after each major snowfall
Fee:	No fee is charged for skiing, but a general entrance fee is required for Yellowstone National Park.
Overview:	The Barronette Trail follows the old Tower-Cooke City, Montana, road through the trees along the eastern base of Barronette Peak. The terrain is gentle and Barronette Peak is magnificent. This trail is not a loop—you will have to ski out and back or spot a car at your destination.
Location:	There are parking areas and trailheads at each end of this trail. The upper (northern) trailhead is located 3 miles southwest of the Yellowstone National Park Northeast Entrance at the northern bridge over Soda Butte Creek. The lower (southern) trailhead is located 6.5 miles southwest of the Yellowstone National Park Northeast Entrance at the southern bridge over Soda Butte Creek. The only winter access to these trailheads is via Mammoth Hot Springs (see chapter overview). From Gardiner, Montana, drive 5 miles south to Mammoth Hot Springs. Turn left on the Mammoth-Tower road and drive 18 miles to Tower Junction. Turn left and drive about 21 miles to the lower (southern) trailhead, or 24 miles to the upper (northern) trailhead. The lower trailhead is about 45 miles from Gardiner and the upper trailhead is about 49 miles from Gardiner.

Description: From the parking area at the upper (northern) trailhead the trail proceeds down the western side of Soda Butte Creek. The trail follows the roadbed of the old Tower-Cooke City highway along the base of Barronette Peak. The trail crosses flat to gently rolling terrain as it passes through a mix of forest and open meadow. The scenery is superb. Barronette Peak (10,442') forms a wall of mountains on your immediate right, Abiathar Peak (10,928') forms a wall of mountains to your left, across Soda Butte Creek.

The trail heads down the flat valley bottom of Soda Butte Creek for 3.5 miles, then terminates at the lower (southern) trailhead. This trailhead is located at the southern bridge over Soda Butte Creek. This trail is not a loop—you will have to ski out and back or spot a car at your destination.

Barronette Peak is named after Jack Barronett. Around the turn of the century when gold mining was booming in Cooke City, Jack Barronett operated a toll bridge over the Yellowstone River near Tower Junction. He was also an Army scout and Yellowstone guide.

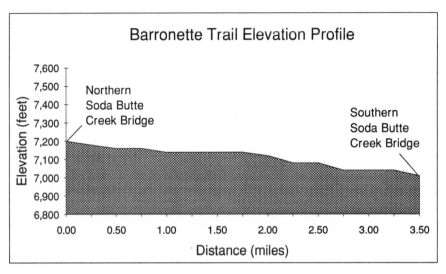

Additional Information: Call the National Park Service at 307-344-2109 (visitor information), or 307-344-7381 (central switchboard). Or write P.O. Box 168, Yellowstone National Park, Wyoming, 82190.

This trail is covered by the U.S. Geological Survey topographical map: Abiathar Peak Quadrangle, WY, 7.5 minute series

Extreme

Difficulty: Extreme

Length: 13 miles one way

Grooming: Skied after each major snowfall

Fee: No fee is charged for skiing, but a general entrance fee is required for Yellowstone National Park.

Overview: A difficult backcountry excursion that normally requires breaking trail. Because of this and because of the length, most skiers take two days to complete the journey. Unless you're prepared for a night of winter camping, this is not the trail for you. Some experienced skiers make it as a day trip, but that is normally in early spring when the days are longer and the snow is firmer.

Location: This trail starts at the Warm Creek Picnic Area 1 mile west of the Northeast Entrance of Yellowstone National Park, 5 miles west of Cooke City, Montana. The only winter access to this trailhead is via Mammoth Hot Springs (see chapter overview). From Gardiner, Montana, drive 5 miles south to Mammoth Hot Springs. Turn left on the Mammoth-Tower road and drive 18 miles to Tower Junction. Turn left and drive about 28 miles to the Warm Creek Picnic Area. The trailhead is about 52 miles from Gardiner, Montana. This trail is not a loop—we recommended you do this trail with friends and that you leave a car at both ends of the trail.

Description: From the parking lot at the Warm Creek Picnic Area, go west along the Tower-Cooke City highway for less than 0.25 mile to the Pebble Creek trailhead, located on the north side of the highway. The trail climbs steeply, gaining 1,000 feet of elevation over the first 1.5 miles. Climbing skins are recommended for this portion of the trail. Avalanche danger on this portion of the trail can be high. Check with rangers at the northeast entrance before skiing this trail.

From its high point of 8,300 feet, the trail descends moderate steep slopes for the next 0.5 mile, until it reaches Pebble Creek. The trail veers left (west) after crossing Peeble Creek, into open meadows walled in on both sides by towering mountains and ridges. The view is spectacular. Cutoff Mountain (10,695') forms the canyon wall on your right, Barronette Peak (10,442') forms the canyon wall to your left.

For the remainder of its route the trail continues through the beautiful Pebble Creek canyon. The trail heads west through open meadows for the next 2 miles before veering left (south) into a mix of forest and meadow. The terrain is gentle to moderately rolling. For the next 5 miles the trail continues south along the valley bottom. The canyon narrows somewhat, the meadows become scarce. At mile 9 (from the trailhead) the trail begins to climb the left (east) side of the canyon for the next 2 miles, until you reach a point nearly 500 feet above the canyon floor. From here the trail takes a steep downhill plunge for the remaining 1.5 miles to Pebble Creek Campground, where you should have previously spotted a vehicle.

We strongly advise that you check local snow conditions before skiing the Pebble Creek Trail. If you plan to spend a night out on the trail, you must obtain the necessary camping permit from a Park Ranger.

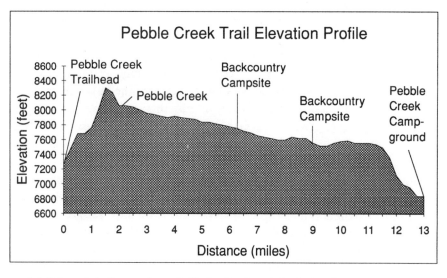

Additional Information: Call the National Park Service at 307-344-2109 (visitor information), or 307-344-7381 (central switchboard). Or write P.O. Box 168, Yellowstone National Park, Wyoming, 82190.

This trail is covered by the U.S. Geological Survey topographical maps:
Cutoff Mountain Quadrangle, MT-WY, 7.5 minute series
Abiathar Peak Quadrangle, WY, 7.5 minute series

Overview: An unmaintained area providing backcountry skiing in a spectacular alpine setting.

Location: The Cooke City/Beartooth Plateau area straddles the Wyoming/Montana border just east of the Northeast Entrance to Yellowstone National Park. The only winter access to Cooke City is via Mammoth Hot Springs (see chapter overview). Cooke City is about 57 miles from Gardiner, Montana.

Description: The Cooke City/Beartooth Plateau area is not a defined ski trail or set of ski trails, but rather an area that provides virtually unlimited opportunities for backcountry skiing. Valley bottoms provide easy to moderate skiing, while the remote alpine expanses of the Beartooth Plateau offer extreme skiing conditions for the advanced and expert skier.

It is beyond the scope of this book to provide detailed descriptions of skiing in the Cooke City/Beartooth Plateau area. Instead, we offer some general comments, and references for obtaining detailed skiing information.

Access can be a problem. The only winter automobile access to Cooke City is via Mammoth Hot Springs (see chapter overview). The Beartooth Highway (Highway 212 between Cooke City and Red Lodge, Montana) is closed from mid-October to the end of May.

The Beartooth Highway is plowed in late May. Since snow lingers here well into July, the Beartooth Highway typically provides automobile access for a month of spring skiing.

Snowmobile lifts to backcountry skiing sites can be arranged through the Cooke City Bike Shack. Snowmobile rentals are also available in Cooke City.

Avalanche danger can be high. Be sure to check on local snow conditions. Ski this area with a friend and leave information with a friend concerning your planned route and return time. Avalanche transmitters and climbing skins are strongly advised for skiing in steep terrain.

Additional Information: An informative and entertaining discussion of backcountry skiing in the Cooke City area is: *Nine Months of Winter; a Nordic Skier's Guide to Northeast Yellowstone and the Cooke City Area.* Available from Larry Fahlberg. P.O. Box 1131, Cooke City, MT 59020.

For information on snowmobile shuttles to backcountry ski sites, contact: The Cooke City Bike Shack, Highway 212, Cooke City, MT 59020, (406) 838-2412.

Campanula Springs/Fir Ridge Ski Trails
General Overview

Solitude and powder snow make the Campanula Springs/Fir Ridge neighborhood pleasant. (Photo by Ken Olsen.)

This area has one ski trail, a lot of wildlife viewing and gentle slopes for telemark practice. It is a 10-minute drive from West Yellowstone, often has deep, untouched powder and is not heavily used. It's a favorite for a day of solitude and easy skiing.

Campanula Springs Trail

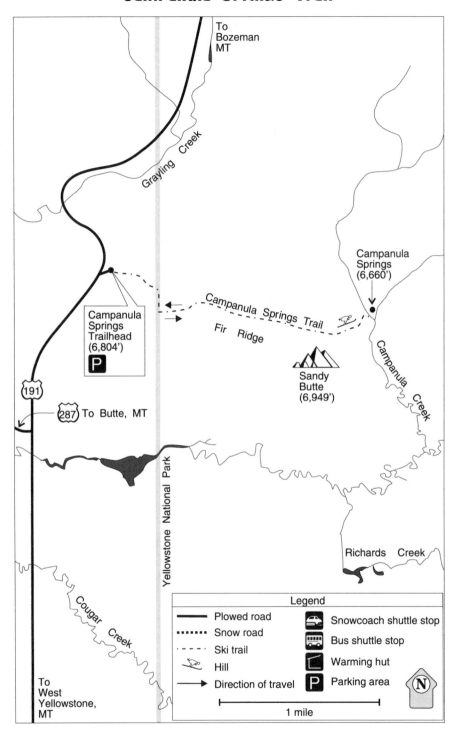

To
Bozeman
MT

Grayling Creek

Campanula
Springs
(6,660')

Campanula Springs Trail

Campanula
Springs
Trailhead
(6,804')

P

Fir Ridge

Sandy
Butte
(6,949')

Campanula Creek

191

287 To Butte, MT

Yellowstone National Park

Richards Creek

To
West
Yellowstone,
MT

Cougar Creek

Legend

———	Plowed road	🚐	Snowcoach shuttle stop
•••••••	Snow road	🚌	Bus shuttle stop
- - - -	Ski trail		Warming hut
🎿	Hill	**P**	Parking area
——➤	Direction of travel		

1 mile

N

Difficulty:	Easy, except for a short, steep hill at the very end
Length:	4 miles round trip
Grooming:	Tracked by skiers
Fee:	None

Easy

Overview: This is a short, mostly level trail that leads to a spring used by wildlife all winter. It is quiet, has a hill perfect for telemark practice and offers a grand view of the Richards Creek drainage. Unlike most area ski trails, this is not a loop.

Location: Follow U.S. Highway 191, the road to Bozeman, Montana, north for about 9.5 miles from West Yellowstone, Montana. As you near the top of a hill, watch for a sign on the right that says "Fir Ridge Cemetery." Turn right into a parking area located among the snowdrifts. If you find yourself driving down a steep grade and crossing Grayling Creek, you have gone too far.

Description: This trail heads east into Yellowstone National Park across a gentle meadow and into a mix of aspen, pine and fir. Follow ski tracks that begin at the north end of the parking lot up a slight incline and soon lead to a trail registry and trail sign.

Of the six trails listed, only the one to Campanula Creek Springs is a ski trail. We recommend you not ski beyond the springs. You'd have to break trail, there are no markers and some of the other trails are difficult in the summer, according to comments we've read in the trail registry.

The tracks head east across an open meadow and to the north side of a tree-topped knob. To the south, you can see a cleared path through the trees that stretches to the horizon. That's the boundary between the Gallatin National Forest and Yellowstone National Park. Open benches also stretch south, descending to a thin line of trees and to Richards Creek. This meandering stream is a haven for elk and buffalo.

The trail continues east through an open meadow, a small stand of trees, and comes to an open hillside on the north side of Fir Ridge. The trail begins to descend gently. The slope increases as the trail gradually draws into a stand of burned trees. The trail drops sharply for the final 100 yards to Campanula Springs. Be prepared to snow plow if you are not confident you can make moderately fast turns among the trees.

Return on the same trail.

Other Fir Ridge Possibilities

If the short trail isn't enough of a challenge or if you've missed the wildlife at the spring, the Fir Ridge area offers pleasant options. As you cross the open hillside, veer right to cross over to the south side of Fir Ridge for pleasant telemark practice in the powder. This is a long, fairly gentle descent perfect for working on confident turns.

It is a short ski south across an open hillside to Richards Creek to get a better view of the wildlife bedded along its banks. You may even find the tracks of other skiers headed that direction. Use great caution in approaching wildlife. While they appear docile, they can easily trample a skier and they are probably more agile in snow than you. One option is to ski in an arc from the first meadow toward Richards Creek, and back to Sandy Butte.

The area has acres of untouched powder snow and pleasant solitude. It is highly recommended on a day you need sunshine and a view, but not extreme physical challenge.

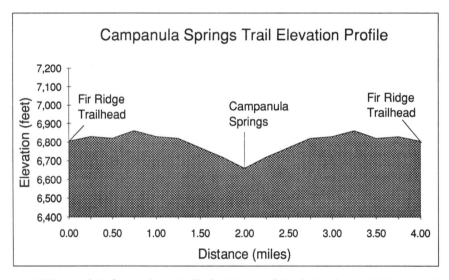

Additional Information: Call the National Park Service at 307-344-2109 (visitor information), or 307-344-7381 (central switchboard). Or write P.O. Box 168, Yellowstone National Park, WY 82190.

This trail is covered by the U.S. Geological Survey topographical map: Richards Creek Quadrangle, MT-WY, 7.5 minute series.

Canyon Ski Trails
General Overview

In January 1887, an intrepid skier pauses near Norris Geyser Basin. (Photo by F. Jay Haynes, courtesy of the Wyoming State Museum.)

Located in the heart of Yellowstone National Park, the Canyon area offers four ski trails, including one along the Grand Canyon of the Yellowstone River, and it has great snow conditions. But you cannot get here by automobile. Your options include snowmobiling from West Yellowstone, Flagg Ranch or Mammoth Hot Springs. West Yellowstone is about 40 miles away, Mammoth Hot Springs 33 miles, and Flagg Ranch is 60 miles away. Though West Yellowstone is a few miles farther than Mammoth Hot Springs, West Yellowstone has more snowmobile rental shops, more motels and more stores that rent skis.

It also is possible to catch a snowcoach to Canyon from West Yellowstone,

Mammoth Hot Springs or Old Faithful. Check locally for scheduling and cost. See elsewhere in this book for a listing of snowcoach operators.

With one exception, trails around Canyon don't cover particularly challenging terrain. There are some telemarking opportunities in the Washburn Hills area and on the Cascade Lake trail.

Cascade Lake Trail

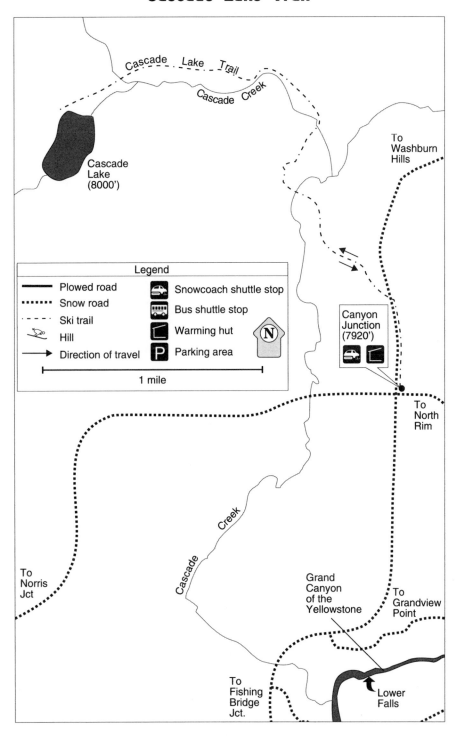

Cascade Lake Trail

Cascade Creek

Cascade Lake (8000')

To Washburn Hills

Legend

——	Plowed road	🚐	Snowcoach shuttle stop
····	Snow road	🚌	Bus shuttle stop
-··-	Ski trail	🏠	Warming hut
🎿	Hill	🅿	Parking area
→	Direction of travel		

N

1 mile

Canyon Junction (7920')

To North Rim

To Norris Jct

Cascade Creek

Grand Canyon of the Yellowstone

To Grandview Point

To Fishing Bridge Jct.

Lower Falls

Roller Coaster, Canyon Rim Trails

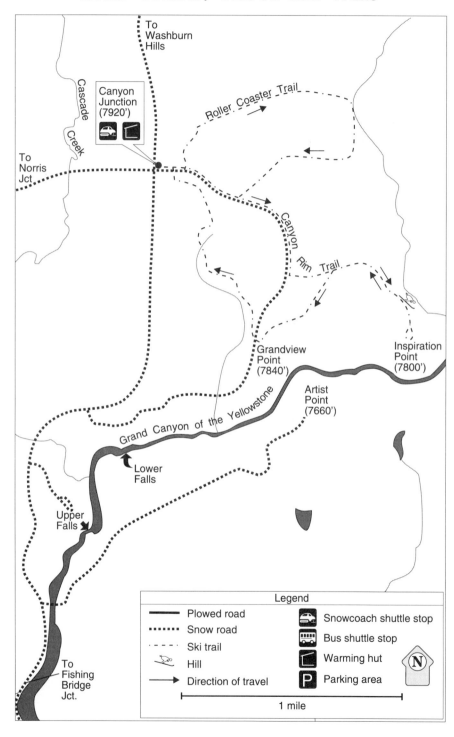

To Washburn Hills

Cascade Creek

Canyon Junction (7920')

To Norris Jct

Roller Coaster Trail

Canyon Rim Trail

Grandview Point (7840')

Inspiration Point (7800')

Artist Point (7660')

Grand Canyon of the Yellowstone

Lower Falls

Upper Falls

To Fishing Bridge Jct.

Legend

—— Plowed road	Snowcoach shuttle stop
···· Snow road	Bus shuttle stop
- - - Ski trail	Warming hut
Hill	Parking area
→ Direction of travel	N

1 mile

Difficulty: Moderate

Length: 6 miles round trip

Grooming: None; skiers must frequently break trail.

Fee: No fee is charged for skiing, but a general entrance fee is required for Yellowstone National Park.

Overview: Cascade Lake is a fairly level trail that traverses both meadow and forest and takes you to the shores of ice-covered Cascade Lake. Its moderate rating comes from its length, not the terrain. Buffalo are common in the meadows and the views of the Washburn Range are outstanding. Be sure to check at the Canyon Warming Hut about avalanche conditions before telemarking.

Location: The trail begins and ends at the Canyon Warming Hut, just northeast of Canyon Junction.

Description: Take the Canyon-Washburn Hills snow road north from the Canyon Warming Hut for about 0.25 mile. The Cascade Lake Trail veers off the snow road on the left side, following a service road for a couple hundred yards before turning right (north) into a lodgepole pine forest.

The trail meanders through the forest and across gentle terrain for approximately 0.25 mile before emerging into meadows.

You may see buffalo throughout the meadows. Avoid these wild animals at all costs. More Yellowstone Park visitors are injured by buffalo than by bear. Buffalo can move surprisingly fast, even in snow. Park regulations require that you keep at least 25 yards from buffalo and other wildlife.

The trail skirts the meadow in a northerly direction for another 0.75 mile, then turns left (west). The trail enters a lodgepole pine forest. It turns right and briefly heads up an open draw.

Depending on snow depth, you may encounter a trail sign. This is the half-way point. Orange markers are visible both to the left and right. Go right.

The trail climbs briefly and re-enters the trees. The terrain is gently rolling. After approximately 0.5 mile the trail emerges from the trees into another open meadow.

From here, the trail takes a straight shot across the meadow. The lake is at the far end of this meadow. The hills near the lake provide decent telemark practice for the more experienced skier. Do **not** ski on the lake.

To return, retrace your steps.

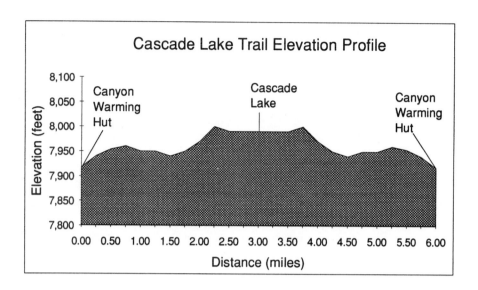

Additional Information: Call the National Park Service at 307-344-2109 (visitor information), or 307-344-7381 (central switchboard). Or write P.O. Box 168, Yellowstone National Park, Wyoming, 82190.

This trail is covered by the U.S. Geological Survey topographical maps:
Canyon Village Quadrangle, WY, 7.5 minute series
Crystal Falls Quadrangle, WY, 7.5 minute series
Cook Peak Quadrangle, WY, 7.5 minute series

Difficulty: Moderate

Length: 4.5 miles round trip

Moderate

Grooming: Machine-groomed for track skiing where the trail follows the North Rim snow road.

Fee: No fee is charged for skiing, but a general entrance fee is required for Yellowstone National Park.

Overview: The Canyon Rim Trail offers magnificent views of the Grand Canyon of the Yellowstone and some fairly fast downhill skiing. Parts of the trail also wind through dense trees and past the summer cabins. Overall, it is the best ski trail in the Canyon area.

Location: The trail begins and ends at the Canyon Warming Hut, just northeast of Canyon Junction.

Description: Head east from the Canyon Warming Hut on the trail that follows the North Rim Drive to Inspiration Point. This portion of the trail consists of a groomed ski trail on the edge of the snow road. Keep alert for snowmobile traffic. The trail begins on the level then climbs through dense lodgepole pine. The trail drops, levels out and draws up to the Inspiration Point turnoff. Take a hard left and begin climbing. The trail levels briefly, climbs a short distance, and then begins a sharp descent. This is a fast ski, especially if icy.

The snow road branches. Stay right, and in a short distance you come to Inspiration Point on the Grand Canyon of the Yellowstone. The 24-mile-long canyon is from 1,500 to 4,000 feet wide and from 750 to 1,200 feet deep. From Inspiration Point you can hear the Lower Falls, 1.5 miles away.

The yellow, red and white hues of the canyon wall are beautiful.

From here the trail backtracks up the steep incline you just zipped down. About 0.6 mile farther the trail takes a sharp left onto an abandoned road and leads you down a mostly level lodgepole pine corridor.

In about 0.5 mile, the trees will thin on the left and you can see the canyon again. The trail begins to follow the canyon rim. Start watching for orange markers on trees. **WARNING:** Do not ski too close to the canyon edge. Remove your skis anytime you venture out to look at the canyon and be very cautious! The snow cornices on the edge collapse easily and could send you into the canyon.

You'll soon hear the roar of the Lower Falls. The trail climbs again and the canyon view becomes more and more spectacular as you come to Grandview Overlook. The upper 2.5 miles of the canyon are said to be the most colorful, due to the interaction between hot springs and iron compounds in the canyon walls.

From Grandview Overlook the trail leads directly away from the canyon, following a marked hiking trail back toward Canyon Junction. The trail follows level to gently rolling terrain through dense lodgepole pine. In about 0.5 mile you encounter summer cabins.

Continue past the cabins to the Canyon Lodge and Visitor Center, boarded up for winter. The trail soon ends at the warming hut.

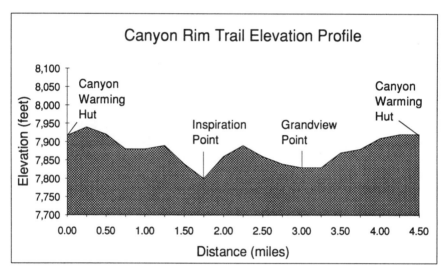

Additional Information: Call the National Park Service at 307-344-2109 (visitor information), or 307-344-7381 (central switchboard). Or write P.O. Box 168, Yellowstone National Park, Wyoming, 82190.

This trail is covered by the U.S. Geological Survey topographical map: Canyon Village Quadrangle, WY, 7.5 minute series

Difficulty:	Moderate
Length:	2.25 miles
Grooming:	None, but skied frequently.

Moderate

Fee: No fee is charged for skiing, but a general entrance fee is required for Yellowstone National Park.

Overview: This trail makes a 2.25-mile loop through a dense lodgepole pine forest across gentle to moderately rolling terrain. Novice to intermediate skiers should enjoy the mixed terrain. Scenery and wildlife are lacking.

Location: The trail begins and ends at the Canyon Warming Hut, just northeast of Canyon Junction.

Description: From the trailhead at the Canyon Warming Hut, the Roller Coaster Trail follows the North Rim snow road east for about 100 yards before turning left onto an unplowed service road. The trail passes just behind the Canyon amphitheater, then goes north along this service road for about 0.3 mile to a small clearing. Along this route, the trail winds through dense lodgepole pine, climbing gradually.

At the clearing, the trail veers right onto a narrow forest path. This path defines a loop that eventually leads back to the North Rim snow road. All along this path you may see signs that point to a campground to the right.

For the next 0.5 mile, the trail climbs over gently rolling hills. The trail begins to gently drop after crossing an unmaintained service road.

You make a 90-degree turn to the right at the farthest point of the loop. The terrain is moderately steep to steep and is downhill. The trail levels out after approximately 0.3 mile.

Another 90-degree turn to the right puts the skier on the final leg of the loop, headed back toward the North Rim snow road. The trail follows moderately rolling hills, trending uphill for the first half of the leg, downhill for the second half.

The trail rejoins the North Rim snow road about 200 yards east of where the loop started. Turn right onto the North Rim snow road to return to the Canyon Warming Hut.

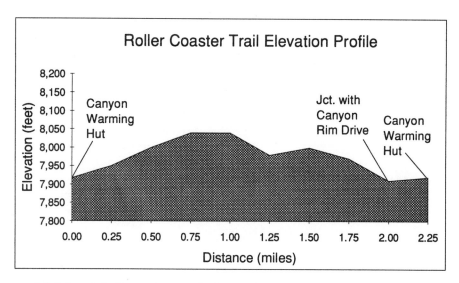

Additional Information: Call the National Park Service at 307-344-2109 (visitor information), or 307-344-7381 (central switchboard). Or write P.O. Box 168, Yellowstone National Park, Wyoming, 82190.

This trail is covered by the U.S. Geological Survey topographical map: Canyon Village Quadrangle, WY, 7.5 minute series

Difficulty: Difficult

Length: Not applicable

Difficult

Grooming: None

Fee: No fee is charged for skiing, but a general entrance fee is required for Yellowstone National Park.

Overview: An unmaintained area providing backcountry skiing on steep, open hillsides for the advanced skier. This is **not** an area for novice skiers.

Location: The Washburn Hills area is 4 miles north of Canyon at the Washburn Hot Springs Overlook. The Canyon snow road dead ends at the Washburn Hot Springs Overlook. It does not continue to Tower Junction.

Description: The Washburn Hills area is not a defined ski trail or set of ski trails, but rather an area that provides off-track, backcountry skiing for experienced skiers.

The left (west) side of the Canyon-Washburn Hills snow road offers long, open hillsides for downhill and telemark skiing. Slopes are steep, almost without exception, increasing in severity as one proceeds up the road toward Dunraven Pass.

Avalanche danger can be high. Be sure to check with a ranger at the Canyon Warming Hut for local snow conditions. Ski this area with a friend and leave information with a friend concerning your planned route and return time. Avalanche transmitters and climbing skins are strongly advised.

Additional Information: Call the National Park Service at 307-344-2109 (visitor information), or 307-344-7381 (central switchboard). Or write P.O. Box 168, Yellowstone National Park, Wyoming, 82190.

This area is covered by the U.S. Geological Survey topographical map:
Mount Washburn Quadrangle, WY, 7.5 minute series

West Yellowstone Ski Trails
General Overview

The West Yellowstone, Montana, area is a wonderful place to cross-country ski. There are two sets of ski trails within walking distance of town and others within a maximum drive of 30 miles over well-maintained roads. Temperatures are generally colder than other skiing areas around Yellowstone National Park. (We recommend your car be equipped with some sort of engine heater before you make your winter visit.) But there is more snow here—up to 160 inches a year.

Frequent snowcoach service and abundant snowmobile rentals make it easier to reach Old Faithful and Canyon ski trails from here than about anywhere else on the edge of Yellowstone National Park.

West Yellowstone also attracts loads of snowmobilers, but that shouldn't dissuade you. You'll hear a lot of them on the streets of town, but most skiing is far away from the sound of these machines.

Hotel rooms are difficult to secure for November, February and around Christmas. Call several months in advance.

West Yellowstone Street Map

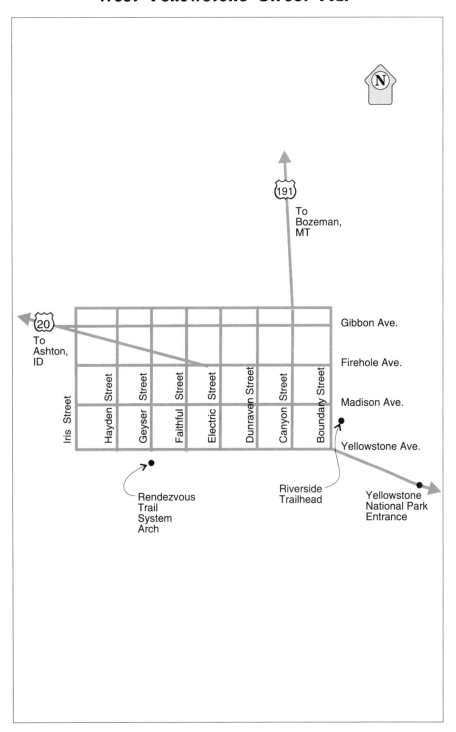

Riverside Trails

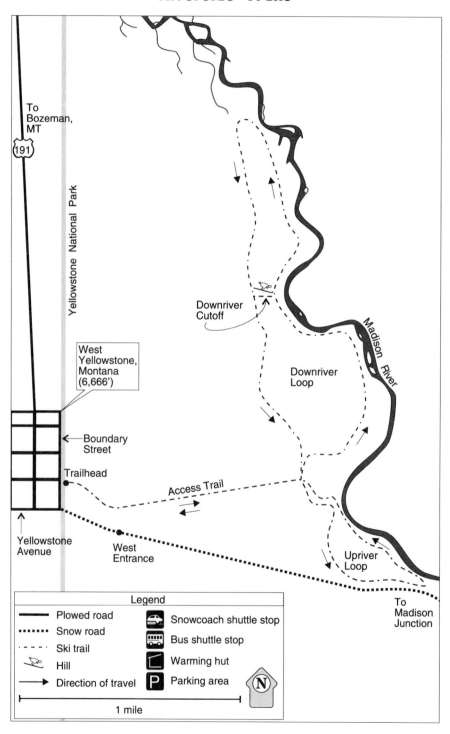

To
Bozeman,
MT

(191)

Yellowstone National Park

West
Yellowstone,
Montana
(6,666')

← Boundary
Street

Trailhead

↑
Yellowstone
Avenue

West
Entrance

Access Trail

Downriver
Cutoff

Downriver
Loop

Madison River

Upriver
Loop

To
Madison
Junction

Legend

——	Plowed road	🚐	Snowcoach shuttle stop
····	Snow road	🚌	Bus shuttle stop
- - -	Ski trail		Warming hut
🎿	Hill	**P**	Parking area
→	Direction of travel		

1 mile

N

Easy

Difficulty: Easy to moderate

Length: Access Trail: 1 mile one way
Upriver Loop: 1.6 miles round trip from trail junction, 3.6 miles round trip from trailhead.
Downriver Loop: 3.7 miles round trip from trail junction, 5.7 miles round trip from trailhead.
Both loops and the access trail total: 7.3 miles round trip from trailhead.

Grooming: Intermittent

Fee: None

Overview: The trail starts at the edge of West Yellowstone and heads into Yellowstone National Park. Since it's close to town, it provides a great place to ski when you sleep late, want to get acquainted with your skis, or don't feel like driving somewhere to start skiing. This trail mostly follows the Madison River, and it's a great place to see waterfowl, buffalo, an occasional elk and a glimpse of what the fire of 1988 did to the Madison River country. The terrain is fairly gentle with an optional short steep hill for telemark practice.

Location: The trail begins and ends on the east side of Boundary Street, near the Madison Avenue intersection in West Yellowstone, Montana.

Description: This trail system takes you into the western edge of Yellowstone National Park. It offers several levels of difficulty depending on the loop you choose. None of the three loops is difficult. But because of the distance, skiing the downriver loop or both loops may not be for beginners.

The **access trail** is a ski-pole straight, mile-long segment. This flat stretch through lodgepole pine forest is perfect for beginners.

In all our visits to the Madison River trails, we have found them groomed only once, but it is rare to have to break trail. This system sees lots of skiers and you can generally count on the trails being in fair condition or better.

About 0.25 mile in, you come to a trail registry. Another 0.75 mile brings you to the center of the figure eight that makes up the Madison River Trails.

Both loops begin here.

From here, watch for signs of elk. On both loops you will see elk tracks across the trail. On one visit, our group watched as a cow elk and her calf struggled through deep snow and cold water to cross the Madison River only a few yards away. Waterfowl are present, though not abundant, on this stretch of the river.

To reach the **upriver loop** take the trail to your right. The loop is a little more than 1.5 miles long. Most of it is easy. The first portion drifts through gently rolling, forested terrain on top of the ridge. Views of the river are sparse here.

About 0.5 mile along, you drop off the ridge on a short, steep, straight run through timber. This is only about 60 yards long. Another 0.3 mile through timber thick with elk tracks brings you to the river. From here the trail crosses relatively level ground along the river bank. At the end of the loop an easy climb to the left brings you back to the beginning of the loops and the access trail.

You may continue along the river and connect with the downriver loop instead. To do so, stay along the river and take the right fork instead of climbing the broad left fork to the main trail.

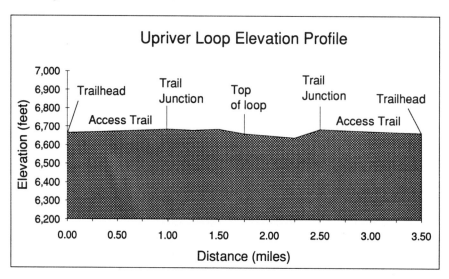

The **downriver loop** is a favorite because of a cutoff about midway that allows you to careen through deep powder or practice telemarking.

To reach the downriver loop from the access trail, veer left at the junction of the loops. Follow the well-packed trail that heads downhill.

This route descends gently through lodgepole pine toward the Madison River and then crosses an open meadow. Dead lodgepole pine, remnants of

The heart of the Riverside Trail System is a pair of loops that take you to wildlife and the banks of the Madison River. (Photo by Ken Olsen.)

the Yellowstone fires of 1988, are visible across the river.

The Gallatin Mountains command the horizon. The Madison River is intriguing, different every year, depending upon how much cold weather has settled on its banks leaving ice jams. Wildlife is common. Take a camera and watch for elk, on their way from Yellowstone Park to haystacks west of the park.

About 1.25 miles from the access trail, an orange sign reads "Cutoff" and points left. The cutoff leads to a short hill for telemark practice.

This hill also is an important landmark for those who do not want to ski the entire loop. If you climb this hill, you can head back to the access trail, 1 mile away. The return trail may not be groomed but it is skied often enough that it is easy to follow. The trail is sporadically marked by orange metal rectangles nailed to trees or stray bits of orange surveyor's tape tied to tree branches.

If you decide to ski the entire downriver loop instead of taking the cutoff, you can stay at the foot of the ridge and the trail will loop back to the top of the hill over 1.3 miles of trail. The 1.3 miles take about 40 minutes for the average skier. While this is the main trail, few skiers use it and it is rarely groomed. You will have to keep sharp watch for occasional orange trail markers nailed to trees.

The trail follows the river for about 0.5 mile. Buffalo sometimes feed along here. Just after a short but sharp incline, the trail veers left and back toward the access trail in dense timber. It stays in the trees for about 0.5 mile before climbing gently to the top of the hill, where the cutoff rejoins the trail.

Stay on top of the hill for another mile to the access trail.

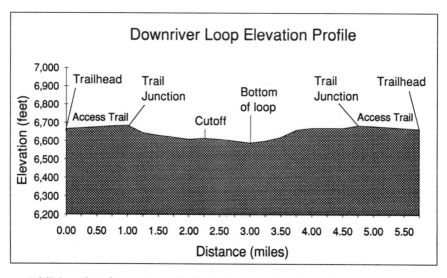

Additional Information: Call the National Park Service at 307-344-2109 (visitor information), or 307-344-7381 (central switchboard). Or write P.O. Box 168, Yellowstone National Park, Wyoming, 82190.

This trail is covered by the U.S. Geological Survey topographical map: West Yellowstone Quadrangle, MT-WY, 7.5 minute series.

Rendezvous Trail System Overview

The Rendezvous system is a smorgasbord of the best maintained trails anywhere in the Yellowstone area. A private, non-profit group from West Yellowstone, Montana, has developed them into a training ground that attracts the U.S. Ski Team, the U.S. Biathlon Association, the World Master's Cross Country Ski Association, and university and European ski teams. These groups usually gather here in November.

Easily reached from West Yellowstone, Rendezvous is unusual in the Yellowstone National Park area because most of the trails are faithfully groomed for both track and skate-style skiing. In some senses, it's like jogging on a paved running path. Approximately 9 miles of trail are groomed all winter.

The scenery is not as spectacular as near Old Faithful and the trails are not as rugged as some. This area receives more than 160 inches of snow and temperatures tend to be colder than other areas in and near the park.

The main loop—called S-Curve—has four cutoffs that allow you to shorten the trip or add a little variety. The system is perfect for moonlight skiing because the well-maintained trails are easy to follow in the semi-darkness.

Rendezvous Trail System

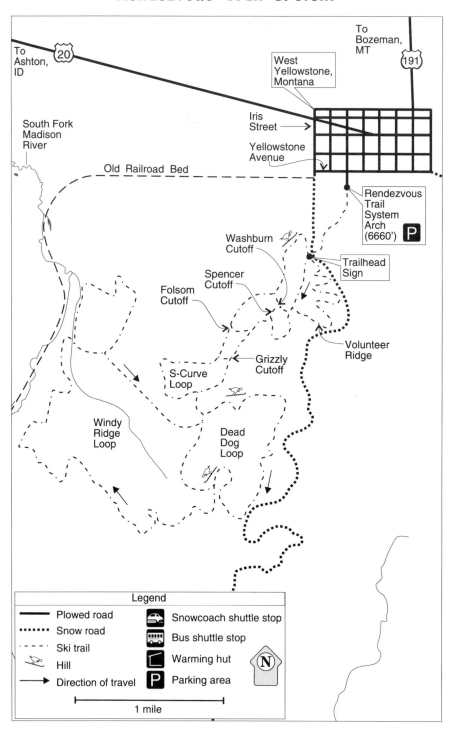

To Ashton, ID

(20)

To Bozeman, MT

(191)

West Yellowstone, Montana

Iris Street →

Yellowstone Avenue

South Fork Madison River

Old Railroad Bed

Rendezvous Trail System Arch (6660') P

Washburn Cutoff

Trailhead Sign

Spencer Cutoff

Folsom Cutoff

Volunteer Ridge

Grizzly Cutoff

S-Curve Loop

Windy Ridge Loop

Dead Dog Loop

Legend

——	Plowed road	🚐	Snowcoach shuttle stop
••••••	Snow road	🚌	Bus shuttle stop
– – –	Ski trail	⌐	Warming hut
🎿	Hill	P	Parking area
→	Direction of travel		

N

1 mile

Difficulty:	Easy to moderate

Easy

Length: 1.2 to 3.6 miles round trip from the trailhead sign, depending upon which cutoff you ski. 2.7 to 5.1 miles round trip from the Rendezvous Arch.

Grooming: Spencer, Washburn and S-Curve loops are groomed regularly, usually several times per week. The other cutoffs are occasionally groomed and are usually tracked by skiers. The trails are groomed to provide a 12-foot wide lane for skate-style skiing and a single track for classic "diagonal" skiing. Trail grooming on all of our visits has been superb.

Fee: No fee December 5th–April 1st. Donations for grooming are accepted in a metal container at the log archway near West Yellowstone.

Overview: S-Curve is a wide, well-packed, rolling trail that travels through doghair lodgepole pine. You can take any of four shortcuts back to the return leg of the main loop. All trails allow one-way travel only. S-Curve is often used by skate skiers who will move faster than traditional skiers.

Location: To reach the trail system, begin at the well-marked log arch about a block south of the intersection of Yellowstone Avenue and Geyser Street in West Yellowstone. (See the town map in this section.) You must follow a 0.7 mile trail from here to reach the starting point for the Rendezvous trails. It is mostly flat, winding through dense lodgepole pine. About 0.5 mile from the beginning, the trail comes to a rail fence and an intersecting snowmobile trail. Check for snowmobiles, which often rip through here at high speed. Cross the snowmobile trail, go up a gentle incline into the trees and you will see the trailhead sign with a map of all of the trails.

Description: This is a 3.6 mile trail with four cutoffs that allow you to shorten your trip. The cutoffs are all clearly signed, but are not always groomed.

From the trail description sign, Washburn loop is 1.1 miles, Spencer Loop is 1.3 miles, Folsom Loop is 1.9 miles, Grizzly Loop is 2.4 miles and S-Curve

Loop is 3.6 miles. Remember that the return trip to town is another 0.7 mile.

As you leave the trail description sign, you will ski up a short, moderately steep hill. The trail rolls through dense lodgepole pine, with a few fairly steep hills. Skiers can avoid the steepest uphill by not completing the entire S-Curve Loop.

Blue signs on the right side of the trail mark Washburn cutoff, then Spencer, then Folsom and then Grizzly. If you decide to do the entire loop, including S-Curve, just stick with the wide, well-groomed main trail. Do not turn when you come to a sign indicating the Dead Dog/Windy Ridge Loop or the biathlon trails.

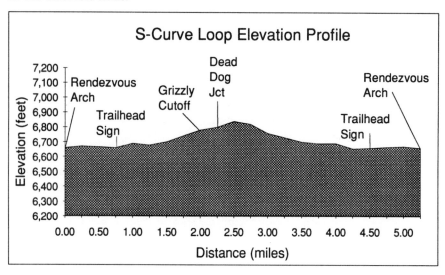

Additional Information: Contact the West Yellowstone Chamber of Commerce at 406-646-7701 or write: P.O. Box 458, West Yellowstone, Montana, 59758.

This trail is covered by the U.S. Geological Survey topographical maps:
West Yellowstone Quadrangle, MT-WY, 7.5 minute series
Madison Arm Quadrangle, MT, 7.5 minute series.

Difficulty:	Moderate

Moderate

Length: 7.1 miles round trip from the trailhead sign, 8.6 miles round trip from the Rendezvous Arch.

Grooming: Weekly. The trail is groomed to provide a 12-foot wide lane for skate-style skiing and a single track for classic "diagonal" skiing.

Fee: No fee December 5th–April 1st. Donations for grooming are accepted in a metal container at the log archway near West Yellowstone.

Overview: This is a 3.4-mile extension of S-Curve Loop that occasionally takes you out of the trees to some better views. There is a sharp, surprise right-hand turn at the bottom of a steep hill about half way through.

Location: Dead Dog Loop begins about 1.8 miles from the trailhead sign, at the southern end of S-Curve Loop.

Description: Dead Dog Loop is a rolling trail that traverses a well-groomed path through lodgepole pine. The trees occasionally open up, affording you pleasing views of the country.

Follow the S-Curve Loop trail from the trail description sign for about 1.8 miles. (See elsewhere in this book for a description of the S-Curve Loop.) As you come to the southern end of the loop, a blue sign on your left will point the way to Dead Dog Loop. Go left.

The trail loops in and out of the trees for more than 3 miles, and includes some exhilarating downhills. Be prepared for an extremely sharp right-hand turn at the bottom of a long, steep hill about halfway along this loop.

Dead Dog Loop rejoins S-Curve Loop after 3.4 miles. You must go left at this junction, because only one-way traffic is allowed. This is S-Curve Loop. It returns you to the trail description sign over 2.5 miles of gentle uphills and downhills.

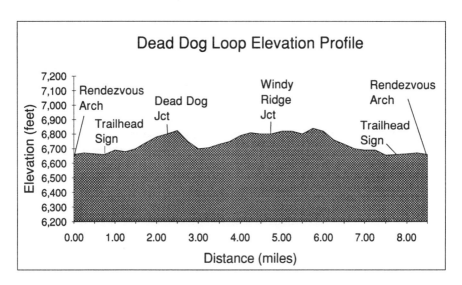

Additional Information: Contact the West Yellowstone Chamber of Commerce at 406-646-7701 or write: P.O. Box 458, West Yellowstone, Montana, 59758.

This trail is covered by the U.S. Geological Survey topographical maps:
West Yellowstone Quadrangle, MT-WY, 7.5 minute series
Madison Arm Quadrangle, MT, 7.5 minute series.

Difficulty:	Moderate

Moderate

Length: 2.6 miles round trip from the trailhead sign, 4.1 miles round trip from the Rendezvous Arch.

Grooming: Daily. The trail is groomed to provide a 12-foot wide lane for skate-style skiing and a single track for classic "diagonal" skiing.

Fee: No fee December 5th–April 1st. Donations for grooming are accepted in a metal container at the log archway near West Yellowstone.

Overview: A short but fun jaunt up and down the pine-covered ridge on the east edge of the Rendezvous trail system.

Location: From the trail description sign, make a sharp left.

Description: This 1.6 mile trail moves around the eastern edge of this trail system, in and out of dense lodgepole pine forest. It rejoins the S-Curve Loop near Washburn cutoff, and you will end up skiing about 2.6 miles if you take Washburn to get back to the trailhead sign.

The trail climbs and descends Volunteer Ridge several times during its route. The ridge is only 50-60 feet tall, but this roller coaster trail provides fun skiing with steep slopes and sharp turns.

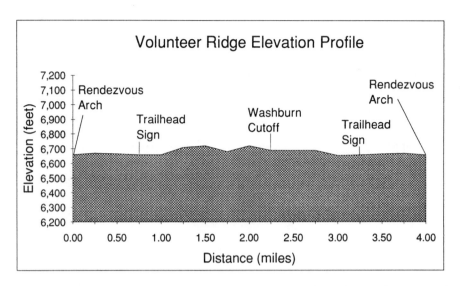

Additional Information: Contact the West Yellowstone Chamber of Commerce at 406-646-7701 or write: P.O. Box 458, West Yellowstone, Montana, 59758.

This trail is covered by the U.S. Geological Survey topographical map: West Yellowstone Quadrangle, MT-WY, 7.5 minute series

Difficulty:	Difficult, due to its length and infrequent grooming

Difficult

Length:	10 miles round trip from the trailhead sign, 11.5 miles round trip from the Rendezvous Arch.
Grooming:	Infrequent
Fee:	No fee December 5th–April 1st. Donations for grooming are accepted in a metal container at the log archway near West Yellowstone.
Overview:	Check with the West Yellowstone Chamber of Commerce before skiing this trail. Windy Ridge Loop is groomed during November and March only. This loop can be difficult to follow when it is ungroomed.
Location:	Windy Ridge Loop begins about 1.8 miles from the trailhead sign, at the southern end of S-Curve Loop.

Description: This trail is infrequently used, except during November and March. **WARNING:** It is fairly easy to get lost on this trail due to its infrequent grooming. We urge you to check with the West Yellowstone Chamber of Commerce before skiing this trail.

Follow the S-Curve Loop trail from the trail description sign for about 1.8 miles. (See elsewhere in this chapter for a description of the S-Curve Loop.) As you come to the southern end of the loop, a blue sign on your left will point the way to Dead Dog Loop. Go left.

In a short distance you come to a second trail junction. Dead Dog Loop goes left, Windy Ridge Loop goes right. For the next 5.5 miles the Windy Ridge Loop trail crosses moderately difficult terrain; ascending and descending several small ridges. Most of the trail is through dense lodgepole pine forest. For roughly half its length the Windy Ridge Loop follows old logging roads.

After 5.5 miles, Windy Ridge Loop rejoins S-Curve Loop at the same point it departed. You must go left at this junction, because only one-way traffic is allowed. This is S-Curve Loop. It returns you to the trail description sign over 2.5 miles of gentle uphills and downhills.

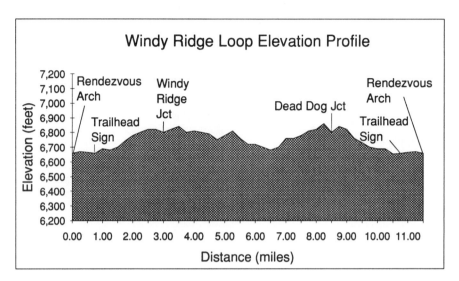

Additional Information: Contact the West Yellowstone Chamber of Commerce at 406-646-7701 or write: P.O. Box 458, West Yellowstone, Montana, 59758.

This trail is covered by the U.S. Geological Survey topographical maps:
West Yellowstone Quadrangle, MT-WY, 7.5 minute series
Madison Arm Quadrangle, MT, 7.5 minute series.

Old Faithful Ski Trails
General Overview

Beautiful thermal features abound in the Old Faithful area. (Photo by Steve Scharosch.)

Don't think of skiing Yellowstone National Park and not skiing the Old Faithful area. This is the best place to see thermal features and wildlife from skis. Period. And watching the namesake, 25,000-year-old geyser spew steam and hot water against the crisp, blue winter sky is enthralling.

There are 11 trails, from short to long, radiating out from the Visitor Center. Trails near Snow Lodge—the restaurant/motel/gift shop open in winter—attract winter hikers and skiers. Ski trails near the lodge are usually riddled with footprints of non-skiers.

The snow melts on short sections of the trail because of the thermal activity and you have to remove your skis. Think about renting skis at Old Faithful or bringing your least favorite pair. Whatever you wear may take some hard use.

WARNING: Foot bridges and walkways may be ice-covered because the steam freezes on them. We recommend you take your skis off and walk across the icy sections. Watch for wet portions of the trail that can cause ice buildup on your skis. Stay on designated trails when viewing the hot pots, pools and geysers. Many of Yellowstone's thermal pools are ringed by thin, delicate crusts covering boiling water. Boardwalks and trails protect visitors from scalding themselves while preserving delicate thermal formations. Please don't defeat their purpose.

You can only reach Old Faithful by snowmobile or snowcoach. Snowcoach service and snowmobile rentals are available in the gateway communities of West Yellowstone and Gardiner, Montana, and Flagg Ranch, Wyoming. West Yellowstone is 30 miles, Mammoth is 51 miles and Flagg Ranch is 44 miles from Old Faithful. (Snowcoach services are listed in the front section of this book).

The disadvantage of rental snowmobiles is that most must be returned by 5 p.m.. Snowmobiling in, skiing and then snowmobiling out makes for a long day. You also will have to rent a sled to carry your skis and they will take additional abuse during that ride. The snowcoaches have ski racks which are easier on your equipment.

One additional warning: Call many months ahead for reservations if you plan to spend the night in the Snow Lodge or one of the cabins. Accommodations are booked six or seven months in advance and there is no waiting list.

In general, we encourage you to ski the areas with thermal features in the morning, when the trees still bear heavy frost, a byproduct of hot steam and freezing temperatures. This is a beautiful area anytime of day. There is not as much solitude as other areas of the park, especially if you stick with the trails close to the visitor center. It is still excellent skiing.

Black Sand Basin and Fern Cascades Trails

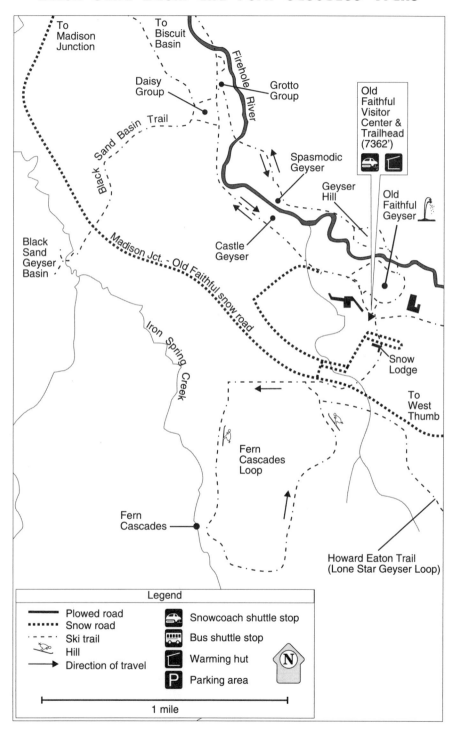

To Madison Junction

To Biscuit Basin

Firehole River

Daisy Group

Grotto Group

Black Sand Basin Trail

Spasmodic Geyser

Old Faithful Visitor Center & Trailhead (7362')

Geyser Hill

Old Faithful Geyser

Black Sand Geyser Basin

Madison Jct. - Old Faithful snow road

Castle Geyser

Snow Lodge

Iron Spring Creek

To West Thumb

Fern Cascades Loop

Fern Cascades

Howard Eaton Trail (Lone Star Geyser Loop)

Legend

—— Plowed road	Snowcoach shuttle stop
······· Snow road	Bus shuttle stop
--- Ski trail	Warming hut
Hill	Parking area
→ Direction of travel	

N

1 mile

Biscuit Basin and Mystic Falls Trails

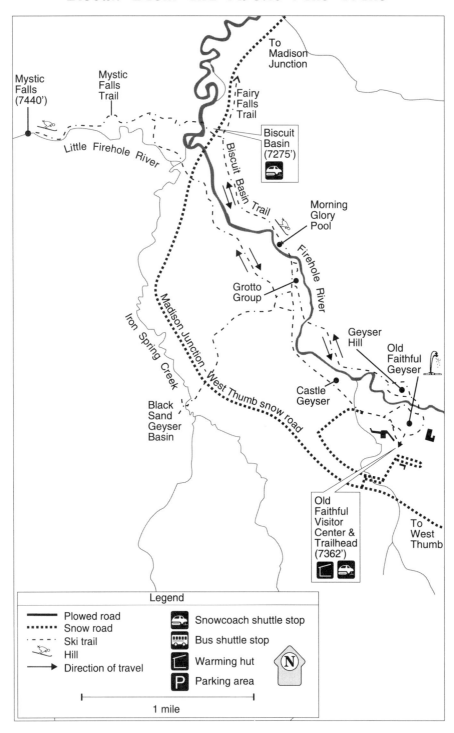

Mystic Falls (7440')

Mystic Falls Trail

To Madison Junction

Fairy Falls Trail

Biscuit Basin (7275')

Little Firehole River

Biscuit Basin Trail

Morning Glory Pool

Firehole River

Grotto Group

Madison Junction

Iron Spring Creek

West Thumb snow road

Geyser Hill

Old Faithful Geyser

Castle Geyser

Black Sand Geyser Basin

Old Faithful Visitor Center & Trailhead (7362')

To West Thumb

Legend

—— Plowed road	Snowcoach shuttle stop
••••• Snow road	Bus shuttle stop
- - - Ski trail	Warming hut
Hill	Parking area
→ Direction of travel	N

1 mile

Lone Star Geyser Trails

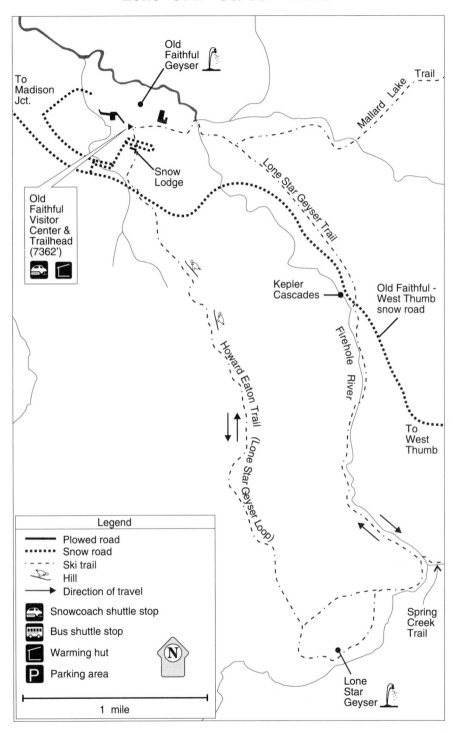

Old Faithful Geyser

To Madison Jct.

Mallard Lake Trail

Snow Lodge

Lone Star Geyser Trail

Old Faithful Visitor Center & Trailhead (7362')

Kepler Cascades

Old Faithful - West Thumb snow road

Firehole River

Howard Eaton Trail (Lone Star Geyser Loop)

To West Thumb

Spring Creek Trail

Lone Star Geyser

Legend

——	Plowed road
······	Snow road
– · –	Ski trail
🎿	Hill
→	Direction of travel
🚐	Snowcoach shuttle stop
🚌	Bus shuttle stop
🏠	Warming hut
P	Parking area

N

1 mile

Mallard Lake, Mallard Creek, Fairy Falls Trails

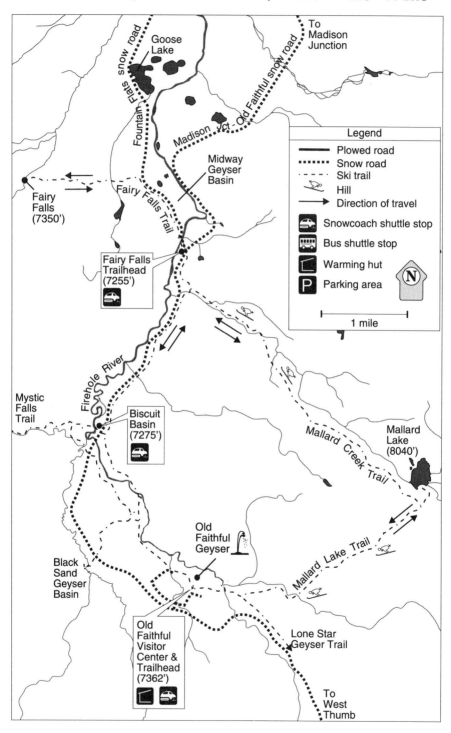

To Madison Junction

Goose Lake

Fountain Flats snow road

Madison Jct - Old Faithful snow road

Midway Geyser Basin

Fairy Falls Trail

Fairy Falls (7350')

Fairy Falls Trailhead (7255')

Legend

——	Plowed road
····	Snow road
– · –	Ski trail
⛷	Hill
→	Direction of travel
🚐	Snowcoach shuttle stop
🚌	Bus shuttle stop
⛺	Warming hut
P	Parking area

N

1 mile

Firehole River

Mystic Falls Trail

Biscuit Basin (7275')

Mallard Creek Trail

Mallard Lake (8040')

Mallard Lake Trail

Old Faithful Geyser

Black Sand Geyser Basin

Lone Star Geyser Trail

Old Faithful Visitor Center & Trailhead (7362')

To West Thumb

Spring Creek and Divide Trails

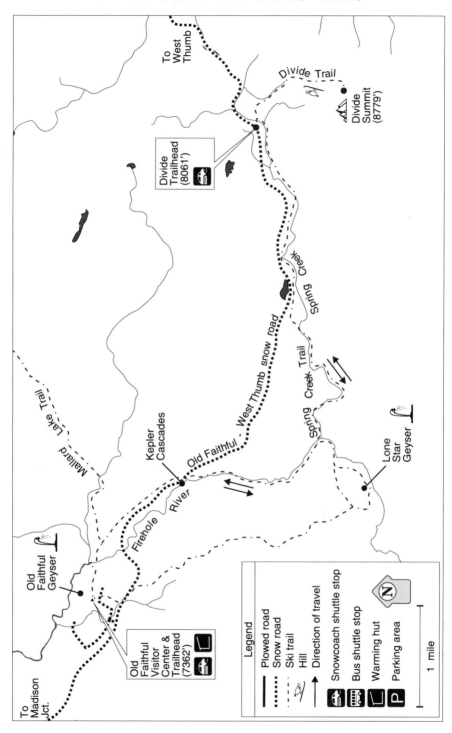

Difficulty:	Easy
Length:	4.25 miles round trip
Grooming:	None, but it is ski-tracked

Easy

Fee: No fee is charged for skiing, but a general entrance fee is required for Yellowstone National Park.

Overview: Like most trails near Old Faithful, this trail is level but the snow can be rough because of hikers and wildlife walking the same path. It is an offshoot of the Biscuit Basin Loop and there are beautiful thermal features, including the Black Sand Pool. The "black sand" is obsidian found in thermal pools throughout the area.

Location: This trail begins in front of the Old Faithful Visitor Center, next to the landmark geyser. A sign will alert you to the next eruption, in case you want to plan your ski trek around it.

Description: Ski northeast from the Visitor Center around the right side of Old Faithful Geyser, cross the Firehole River on a footbridge, and ski up Geyser Hill. The trail is clearly marked, much of it is boardwalk. Thermal pools abound, steaming and bubbling along the trail. Buffalo and elk are common.

The trail soon turns and follows the Firehole River downstream, crossing a thermal flat also frequented by buffalo and elk. The snow is likely pock-marked by their footprints and those of humans. You can take pictures of wildlife, but keep your distance. You will have to remove your skis and walk around bare spots in the trail.

After roughly 0.25 mile you will pass Spasmodic Geyser. Another 0.25 mile brings you to a footbridge crossing the Firehole River, and 0.25 mile beyond that is Grotto Geyser. A trail intersection at Grotto Geyser leads right toward Biscuit Basin, or left toward the Daisy Group and Old Faithful. Go left for a couple hundred yards until you reach the turn off to the Daisy Group. Take a right here.

The trail takes you through meadows and trees, toward the snow vehicle road. Buffalo frequent this area. If you find them using the trail, keep your distance.

In about 0.75 mile you come to the snow vehicle road. Cross it to reach Black Sand Basin. At the basin you may want to remove your skis as you meander across the boardwalks to view Cliff Geyser, Green Spring, Emerald Pool, Rainbow Pool and Sunset Lake.

To return to Old Faithful, retrace your tracks to the Daisy Group turnoff. Going left to Grotto Geyser and then right across the Firehole River will allow you to revisit Geyser Hill. Turning right at the junction will take you past Castle Geyser and on to the Visitor Center.

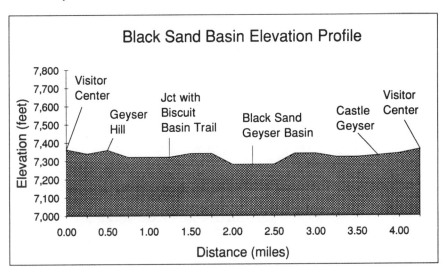

Additional Information: Call the National Park Service at 307-344-2109 (visitor information), or 307-344-7381 (central switchboard). Or write P.O. Box 168, Yellowstone National Park, Wyoming, 82190.

This trail is covered by the U.S. Geological Survey topographical map: Old Faithful Quadrangle, WY, 7.5 minute series

Difficulty:	Easy
Length:	5 miles round trip
Grooming:	Tracked by skiers.

Easy

Fee: No fee is charged for skiing, but a general entrance fee is required for Yellowstone National Park.

Overview: This is an easy trail that features one of the park's most enchanting waterfalls. The Firehole River and portions of the Midway Geyser Basin are passed along the way. Skiing is easy across nearly flat terrain, with minor ups and downs.

Location: The Fairy Falls trailhead is roughly 5 miles north of Old Faithful on the Madison Junction-Old Faithful snow road. Though you can ski to the trailhead from Old Faithful, it adds 10 miles to the trip. Most people take a snowcoach to the trailhead. Ask for a schedule at the Old Faithful Snow Lodge.

Description: The trail starts at the south end exit of the Fountain Flats snow road, roughly 5 miles north of Old Faithful on the Madison Junction-Old Faithful Snow Road.

For the first mile, the trail is on the edge of the Fountain Flats snow road. Watch for heavy snowmobile traffic.

The trail starts with a short flat section leading to a vehicle bridge over the Firehole River. After crossing the river, the trail veers right and proceeds downriver across gentle terrain. A ridge of burned trees is off to your left; the Midway Geyser Basin is on your right. Buffalo and waterfowl are common along the river and geyser basin.

The trail makes an abrupt left turn after 1 mile, leaving the Fountain Flats snow road. Here the trail enters a dense forest of burned lodgepole pine. You continue to parallel the ridge on your left for 1.6 miles to Fairy Falls. Along this entire stretch the terrain is flat to gently rolling.

As you approach Fairy Falls, the trail veers slightly left and climbs a small foothill to the base of the falls. You are treated to a spectacular view of ice, water and snow. The falls make a near-vertical drop of more than 100 feet. Because of its small size, Fairy Creek becomes partially encrusted in a shell of ice.

Return to the trailhead by retracing your steps. If you have not made prior arrangements for a snowcoach pickup, you can ski the 5 miles from the Fairy Falls trailhead to Old Faithful. To do so, cross the Madison Junction-Old Faithful snow road, and proceed to your right (south). After 0.25 mile you will meet the Mallard Creek Loop trail that leads back to Old Faithful. This trail parallels the Madison Junction-Old Faithful snow road for just over 2 miles to a junction with the Biscuit Basin trail, then follows the Biscuit Basin trail for another 2.25 miles to Old Faithful. (The Mallard Creek Loop and Biscuit Basin trails are described elsewhere in this chapter.)

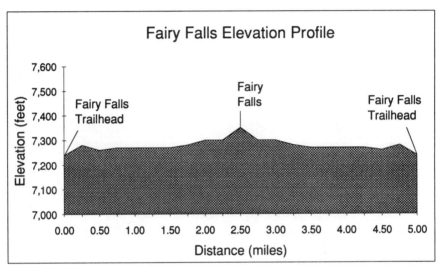

Additional Information: Call the National Park Service at 307-344-2109 (visitor information), or 307-344-7381 (central switchboard). Or write P.O. Box 168, Yellowstone National Park, Wyoming, 82190.

This trail is covered by the U.S. Geological Survey topographical maps:
Old Faithful Quadrangle, WY, 7.5 minute series
Lower Geyser Basin Quadrangle, WY, 7.5 minute series

Biscuit Basin

Difficulty:	Moderate
Length:	5.5 miles round trip
Grooming:	None, but it is well-tracked by skiers
Fee:	No fee is charged for skiing, but a general entrance fee is required for Yellowstone National Park.
Overview:	This is a favorite trail because it provides close-up views of thermal features like Morning Glory pool. Wildlife are abundant. At the thermal pools on the north end of the trail, Canada geese often warm themselves near the steam. The trail is essentially flat, with minor ups and downs.
Location:	This trail officially begins across the road from the Snow Lodge. It is easier to start at the Old Faithful Visitor Center, near the Old Faithful geyser. The visitor center also is the starting point for the Black Sand Basin Trail. Look for a sign that will alert you to the next eruption of Old Faithful, in case you want to plan your ski trek around it.

Description: Ski northeast around the right side of Old Faithful Geyser, cross the Firehole River on a footbridge, and proceed up Geyser Hill. The trail is clearly marked; much of it is boardwalk. Thermal features abound, steaming and bubbling along the trail. Buffalo and elk are often seen on Geyser Hill and along much of the trail.

The trail soon turns and follows the Firehole River downstream, crossing a thermal flat also frequented by buffalo and elk. The trail may be pockmarked by the footprints of humans and wildlife. Take pictures of wildlife, but keep your distance. You will have to remove your skis and walk around bare spots in the trail.

After roughly 0.25 mile you will pass Spasmodic Geyser. Another 0.25 mile brings you to a footbridge crossing the Firehole River, and 0.25 mile beyond that is Grotto Geyser. A trail intersection at Grotto Geyser leads right toward Biscuit Basin, or left toward the Daisy Group and Old Faithful. Go right.

The trail passes in and out of a tree-lined corridor. A few streams, kept running by an endless supply of hot water, weave by the trail.

You cross the Firehole River in a little more than 0.75 mile, and soon reach Morning Glory Pool. A short climb through a dense forest of burned lodgepole pine takes you to Artemisia Geyser at the lower end of Biscuit

Basin. The "biscuits"—the result of thermal deposits—were wiped out by the 1959 Yellowstone-area earthquake. From here the trail proceeds down a gentle grade, passing several small thermal features in Biscuit Basin before turning left to cross the snow road.

After crossing the road the trail goes across a footbridge on the Firehole River, then across a boardwalk and past Shell Geyser and Sapphire Pool.

To return to Old Faithful you may retrace your steps, or take an alternate loop trail for a change of scenery.

To return to Old Faithful on the loop trail, go across the Biscuit Basin boardwalk and to its far side. Just beyond is the junction. Going straight will take you to Mystic Falls, a left will take you back to Old Faithful. Go left.

The trail heads through a small stand of lodgepole pine and out into the meadows of the Little Firehole River. You cross the river on a footbridge, and soon cross the snow road. From here the trail proceeds through alternating meadows and forest for 1 mile, then reconnects with the main Biscuit Basin Trail near Grotto Geyser. Turn right to reach Old Faithful in another mile.

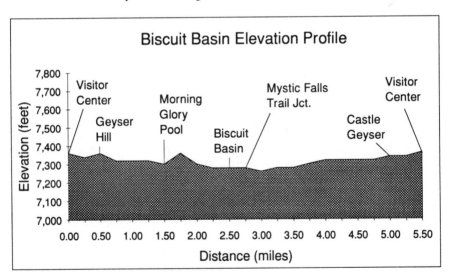

Additional Information: Call the National Park Service at 307-344-2109 (visitor information), or 307-344-7381 (central switchboard). Or write P.O. Box 168, Yellowstone National Park, Wyoming, 82190.

This trail is covered by the U.S. Geological Survey topographical map: Old Faithful Quadrangle, WY, 7.5 minute series

Lone Star Geyser

Difficulty:	Moderate
Length:	9 miles round trip

Moderate

Grooming: Periodically machine-groomed for both skate skiing and traditional cross-country skiing on the 2.5 mile section from Kepler Cascades to Lone Star Geyser. Skier tracked on all other portions.

Fee: No fee is charged for skiing, but a general entrance fee is required for Yellowstone National Park.

Overview: This is a scenic ski to one of the area's premier thermal features. Although there is some climbing early on, the terrain is gentle overall. This trip includes skiing past the beautiful Kepler Cascades and along the Firehole River.

Location: The trail begins at the Old Faithful Snow Lodge.

Description: Don't confuse this trail with the Lone Star Geyser Loop, a more difficult journey described later in this section.

To hook up with the Lone Star Geyser Trail, look for the sign across from the Snow Lodge that marks its beginning. This also is the starting leg of the Mallard Lake Trail.

Follow the trail to the right, around the Old Faithful cabins to the Firehole River. After crossing the river, the trail forks, with the Mallard Lake trail going to the left. Stay right.

The trail climbs through forest for 0.5 mile, following an old road cut that leads to the Old Faithful-West Thumb snow road. From here the trail parallels the snow road for another 0.5 mile, crossing moderate terrain. The trail turns right and crosses the snow road at Kepler Cascades. Take a minute to enjoy the falls.

The trail leaves Kepler Cascades and continues along the east bank of the Firehole River to a junction with an old service road. Watch for buffalo, elk and waterfowl.

From the junction, the trail follows the level service road for 2.5 miles to Lone Star Geyser. This section of the trail is periodically machine-groomed for both skate-style and traditional cross-country skiing. For the first 0.5 mile of this section the trail follows the Firehole River upstream through a forested flat. After crossing the Firehole River, the trail parallels the river for another mile, travelling through a small canyon. The canyon ends at a junction with the Spring Creek Trail. Go right to continue to Lone Star Geyser, 0.75 mile farther.

The geyser gives 30-minute shows about every three hours, and it's a great place to rest and snack.

Return to Old Faithful by the same route.

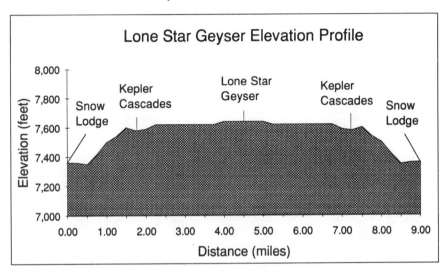

Additional Information: Call the National Park Service at 307-344-2109 (visitor information), or 307-344-7381 (central switchboard). Or write P.O. Box 168, Yellowstone National Park, Wyoming, 82190.

This trail is covered by the U.S. Geological Survey topographical map: Old Faithful Quadrangle, WY, 7.5 minute series

A skier rests in the midday sun and steam. (Photo by Ken Olsen.)

Difficulty: Difficult

Length: 9 miles

Difficult

Grooming: Periodically machine-groomed for both skate skiing and traditional cross-country skiing on the 2.5 mile section from Kepler Cascades to Lone Star Geyser. Skier-tracked on all other portions.

Fee: No fee is charged for skiing, but a general entrance fee is required for Yellowstone National Park.

Overview: This loop has the same great views of Kepler Cascades and the Firehole River as the Lone Star Geyser Trail. The difference is that this route returns to Old Faithful via the Howard Eaton hiking trail, which involves difficult downhill stretches. Check snow conditions at the Old Faithful Visitor Center. If the Howard Eaton Trail is icy, we recommend you not ski it.

Location: The trail begins at the Old Faithful Snow Lodge.

Description: You can ski this trail in either direction, but we recommend doing it clockwise. This will help you avoid steep climbs and tangling with skiers negotiating the sometimes icy hills from the other direction.

Start across from the Old Faithful Snow Lodge, where the sign marks the beginning of the Lone Star Geyser Trail.

Follow the trail to the right, around the Old Faithful cabins to the Firehole River. After crossing the river, the trail forks, with the Mallard Lake trail going to the left. Stay right to go to Lone Star Geyser.

The trail climbs through forest for 0.5 mile, following an old road cut that leads to the Old Faithful-West Thumb snow road. From here the trail parallels the snow road for another 0.5 mile, crossing moderate terrain. The trail turns right and crosses the snow road at Kepler Cascades. Take a minute to enjoy the falls.

The trail leaves Kepler Cascades and continues along the east bank of the Firehole River to a junction with an old service road. Watch for buffalo, elk and waterfowl.

From here the trail follows the level service road for 2.5 miles to Lone Star Geyser. This section of the trial is periodically machine-groomed for both skate-style and traditional cross-country skiing. For the first 0.5 mile of this

103

section the trail follows the Firehole River upstream through a forested flat. After you cross the Firehole River on a bridge, the trail continues to parallel the river for another mile, travelling through a small canyon. The canyon ends at a junction with the Spring Creek Trail. Stay right at the junction to continue on to Lone Star Geyser, 0.75 mile farther.

The geyser gives 30-minute shows about every three hours, and it's a great place to rest and snack.

From the geyser, the trail heads southwest for 0.25 mile, then makes a sharp right turn to the north. The trail soon forks. The right fork leads back to the Lone Star Geyser trail you followed on the outward journey. Stay left to return to Old Faithful via the loop trail (Howard Eaton Trail).

The trail climbs gradually through trees, many of them scarred by the fires of 1988, for about 1.3 miles. You top out on a broad hill, then begin a challenging mile-long downhill run. Some of this is extremely steep and includes sharp curves as it sends you bulleting toward Old Faithful. If you aren't confident of your ability to control your skis, or if the snow is icy, avoid this run.

Shortly after the trail levels, you join the Fern Cascades Loop and follow it to the right, across the snow vehicle road, to Old Faithful.

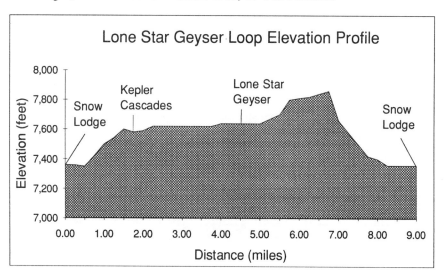

Additional Information: Call the National Park Service at 307-344-2109 (visitor information), or 307-344-7381 (central switchboard). Or write P.O. Box 168, Yellowstone National Park, Wyoming, 82190.

This trail is covered by the U.S. Geological Survey topographical map: Old Faithful Quadrangle, WY, 7.5 minute series

Difficulty:	Difficult	
Length:	8 miles one way	**Difficult**
Grooming:	Tracked by skiers	

Fee: No fee is charged for skiing, but a general entrance fee is required for Yellowstone National Park.

Overview: This is a beautiful journey that follows Spring Creek for about 4 miles before joining the Lone Star Geyser Trail. Like many trails in the area, its difficulty depends on snow conditions. Check with a ranger before starting out.

Location: Take the snowcoach from Old Faithful south 7 miles to the Spring Creek/Divide trailhead.

Description: The trail drops briefly from the south side of the snow vehicle road and then begins climbing. You cross Spring Creek about 100 feet from the road and continue climbing for about 0.3 mile.

A sign points you right to continue on the Spring Creek Trail. The trail starts a long, rolling journey along the creek that can be treacherous if icy. You'll encounter your first footbridge about 1 mile from the first junction, and you'll cross the creek a number of times. Be prepared for ice on the footbridges almost any time.

The trail follows a narrow gorge for the next couple of miles. The terrain is rolling.

Eventually you leave the gorge, cross the Firehole River and link up with the Lone Star Geyser Trail. Go right to return to Old Faithful. Go left to see the geyser, which goes off about every 3 hours for 30 minutes at a stretch.

Even if you choose to go to the geyser, we recommend you return to Old Faithful via the Lone Star Geyser Trail instead of continuing west and then north to the Howard Eaton Trail. The Howard Eaton stretch includes challenging downhill stretches that are more difficult to negotiate if you are tired from your run along Spring Creek. The Howard Eaton Trail should be avoided if icy. See elsewhere in this chapter for discussion of the Lone Star Geyser Trail and Lone Star Geyser Loop Trail.

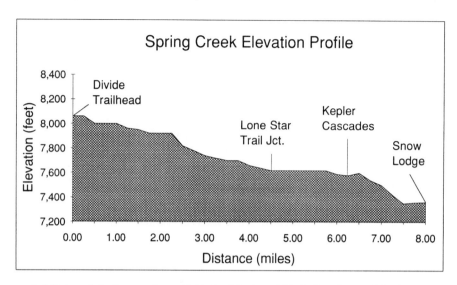

Additional Information: Call the National Park Service at 307-344-2109 (visitor information), or 307-344-7381 (central switchboard). Or write P.O. Box 168, Yellowstone National Park, Wyoming, 82190.

This trail is covered by the U.S. Geological Survey topographical maps:
Old Faithful Quadrangle, WY, 7.5 minute series
Craig Pass Quadrangle, WY, 7.5 minute series

Difficulty:	Difficult	
Length:	7 miles round trip	**Difficult**
Grooming:	Tracked by skiers	

Fee: No fee is charged for skiing, but a general entrance fee is required for Yellowstone National Park.

Overview: This is basically the Biscuit Basin Trail with an additional 1-mile climb to the falls. While the falls are beautiful, this trail tends to be icy. Because it also is narrow, there is little room for error when negotiating the steep slopes above the creek. You cannot ski all the way to the falls, and you might consider walking from near the end of the Mystic Falls trail. (Please don't walk in ski tracks.)

Location: This trail officially begins across the road from the Snow Lodge. It is easier to begin near the Old Faithful Visitor Center.

Description: Follow the Biscuit Basin Trail to its northernmost end, according to the directions earlier in this chapter. When you reach Biscuit Basin, keep going to the far end of the boardwalk and you will see the Mystic Falls trail sign just beyond.

The trail begins climbing gently and forks in a short distance. The left branch returns you to Old Faithful. Stay right. The trail begins to get steeper and winds through dense forest, paralleling the Little Firehole River. Keep an eye out for skiers who may be coming down the trail. From here to the falls, the trail crosses steep hillsides that can be subject to avalanches. Check with rangers at the Old Faithful Ranger Station for current snow conditions.

About 0.25 mile from the falls, the trail rounds a corner to the right and emerges onto an open hillside. This slope is commonly bare due to its southern exposure and underground thermal activity. Depending on the trail condition and your ability, you may want to leave your skis here and continue the rest of the way by foot. The falls are visible just around the corner.

A series of steep switchbacks may be visible leading up the open hillside and toward the crest of the falls. We would discourage anyone but the most experienced skiers from attempting these switchbacks. The view of the falls is just as spectacular from the lower slopes.

The falls are large, cascading down several benches. The volume of water in the Little Firehole River keeps them flowing all winter. Large sheets and mounds of ice form on the surrounding rocks. To return, retrace your steps to Biscuit Basin. Be careful on the downhill slopes, as the trail is narrow with little room for error. From Biscuit Basin you may return to Old Faithful via two different routes. See the return portion of the Biscuit Basin Trail description for more information.

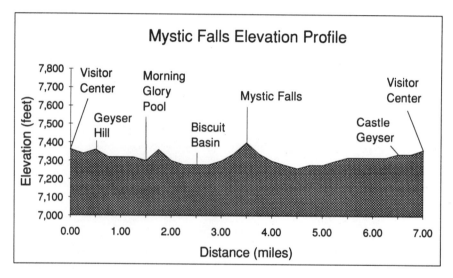

Additional Information: Call the National Park Service at 307-344-2109 (visitor information), or 307-344-7381 (central switchboard). Or write P.O. Box 168, Yellowstone National Park, Wyoming, 82190.

This trail is covered by the U.S. Geological Survey topographical map: Old Faithful Quadrangle, WY, 7.5 minute series

Mystic Falls drops along snow- and ice-encrusted banks. (Photo by Steve Scharosch.)

Difficulty:	Difficult
Length:	3 miles

Difficult

Grooming:	Tracked by skiers
Fee:	No fee is charged for skiing, but a general entrance fee is required for Yellowstone National Park.
Overview:	This is an out-and-back trail that climbs to the continental divide and the former site of a fire lookout. The lookout was removed in 1991, but from the trail just below the lookout you still have a nice view of the park, including its second biggest lake—Shoshone. If you have climbing skins, bring them. Snowcoach is the most common means to get to the trailhead. But a popular return route is to ski Spring Creek Trail back to Old Faithful.
Location:	Getting to the Divide Trail is as easy as taking a snowcoach. These lumbering creatures will drop you at the trailhead about 7 miles east of Old Faithful, near the Continental Divide. Inquire at the Old Faithful Snow Lodge concerning snowcoach scheduling.

Description: The first few feet of this trail are all downhill. The next 1.6 miles are mostly uphill. At about 100 feet from the trailhead, you cross Spring Creek. Soon, at 0.3 mile, you pass Spring Creek Trail that takes off to the right. A sign at this junction indicates that the end of the trail is another 1.4 miles.

From here the trail climbs through a series of small forested draws to a saddle at a little more than 1 mile from the trailhead. The trail goes to the right along the saddle, but if you slip off trail to the left, you can see Shoshone Lake and the Red Mountains beyond.

From the saddle you continue climbing to a clearing at the top of the mountain. Don't hunt for the lookout tower; it was removed in 1991.

The return trip is challenging and fast. If you're planning on taking Spring Creek Trail (see elsewhere in this guide for information on the Spring Creek Trail) back to Old Faithful, go left at the junction. Otherwise, continue to the trailhead to meet your pre-arranged snowcoach shuttle.

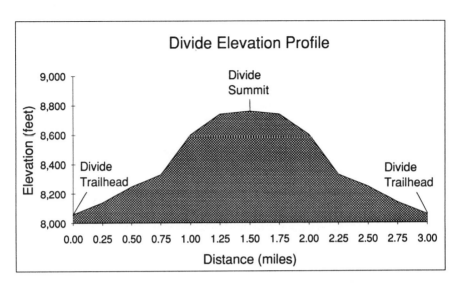

Additional Information: Call the National Park Service at 307-344-2109 (visitor information), or 307-344-7381 (central switchboard). Or write P.O. Box 168, Yellowstone National Park, Wyoming, 82190.

This trail is covered by the U.S. Geological Survey topographical maps:
Old Faithful Quadrangle, WY, 7.5 minute series
Craig Pass Quadrangle, WY, 7.5 minute series

Fern Cascades

Difficulty: Difficult

Length: 3 miles

Grooming: Tracked by skiers

Difficult

Fee: No fee is charged for skiing, but a general entrance fee is required for Yellowstone National Park.

Overview: This is a mostly easy loop, close to Old Faithful with a variety of terrains. It earns its difficult rating because of a killer climb near the trailhead.

Location: Begins from the Old Faithful Snow Lodge.

Description: This is a one-way loop that goes counter-clockwise. The trail starts at the Old Faithful Snow Lodge, proceeding south. The trail crosses the Old Faithful-West Thumb snow road, then turns right. Look for arrows indicating the start of the one-way loop.

After crossing the snow road, the trail heads through a Park Service compound. As you reach the end of the compound, the trail turns abruptly left and starts to climb. The trail climbs steeply across a forested hillside for the next 0.5 mile. Iron Spring Creek canyon is on your right.

The trail tops out, then continues across rolling terrain for a short distance to Fern Cascades. The Cascades are a small waterfall on Iron Spring Creek. They can be viewed from an overlook off the trail. Trying to ski to the overlook is foolhardy. Take off your skis and—even on foot—approach the overlook carefully. Please don't walk on the ski trail.

From the Cascades, the trail veers left and continues for 0.75 mile across the rolling plateau. Here the trail passes through forest burned by the 1988 fires.

As you near the end of the loop, you are rewarded with a fast downhill run along a utility road back to where you started. Just before you reach the start of the loop, you pass a junction with the Lone Star Geyser Loop trail (Howard Eaton Trail) on your right.

At the loop junction turn right to cross the snow road and return to Old Faithful.

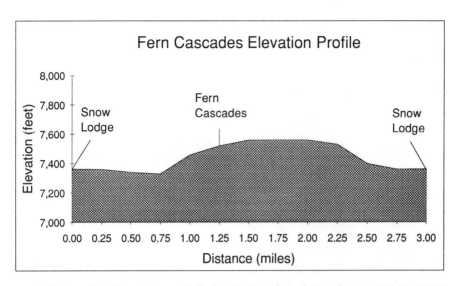

Additional Information: Call the National Park Service at 307-344-2109 (visitor information), or 307-344-7381 (central switchboard). Or write P.O. Box 168, Yellowstone National Park, Wyoming, 82190.

This trail is covered by the U.S. Geological Survey topographical map: Old Faithful Quadrangle, WY, 7.5 minute series

Trees near thermal pools are wrapped in heavy frost. (Photo by Steve Scharosch.)

Difficulty:	Difficult
Length:	7 miles
Grooming:	Tracked by skiers
Fee:	No fee is charged for skiing, but a general entrance fee is required for Yellowstone National Park.
Overview:	This is a challenging and varied out-and-back trail into the edges of Yellowstone's backcountry. For those who like fast, challenging runs, this trail offers you an almost unparalleled 800 feet of elevation gain and loss. It also offers plenty of solitude.
Location:	Begins from the Old Faithful Snow Lodge.

Difficult

Description: Follow the Mallard Lake/Lone Star Geyser trails as they leave the Snow Lodge. Ski around the Old Faithful cabins to the Firehole River. Cross the river on the footbridge.

The trail forks here. Go left, pulling away from the river. The trail takes you into timber burned during the fires of 1988, and then past the Pipeline Group of fumaroles. The steaming pots are beautiful and intriguing, but don't ski off the trail: the ground is soft around them and the water deathly hot.

Here the trail begins a steep climb up the first of a series of plateaus. On top, you cross gently rolling terrain. The blackened "dog hair" lodgepole pines are in stark contrast to the white snow. Much of the length of this trail is through burned trees.

As you near the lake, the trail takes you around the left side of a canyon. Here the trail is narrow and steep. Near the head of the canyon, the trail passes a field of boulders and then goes through a pass to the unburned country on the other side. Once through the pass, you're in the Mallard Lake drainage.

The trail here rolls past small meadows, with occasional climbs. At 3.2 miles, a sign indicates the junction of Mallard Lake and Mallard Creek trails. Stay right to go to the lake. At this point you are at about 8,100 feet.

The trail drops from here to Mallard Lake. It is possible to camp here, but a backcountry camping permit is required. This must be picked up in person at Old Faithful Ranger Station. The permit can be picked up 48 hours in advance.

The return trip can be very fast, especially in the canyon where the trail is narrow and steep.

115

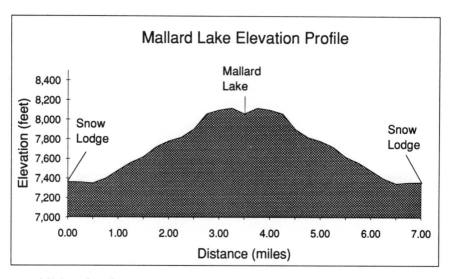

Additional Information: Call the National Park Service at 307-344-2109 (visitor information), or 307-344-7381 (central switchboard). Or write P.O. Box 168, Yellowstone National Park, Wyoming, 82190.

This trail is covered by the U.S. Geological Survey topographical map: Old Faithful Quadrangle, WY, 7.5 minute series

Difficulty: Difficult to extreme

Length: 12 miles

Difficult

Grooming: Occasionally tracked by skiers

Fee: No fee is charged for skiing, but a general entrance fee is required for Yellowstone National Park.

Overview: This is a long trip suitable only for the experienced skier. It takes in portions of the Mallard Lake and Fairy Falls/Biscuit Basin trails. Wildlife abounds as does just about every possible skiing terrain. Check with the Old Faithful Visitor Center before venturing out on this trail since snow conditions make a vast difference in its level of difficulty.

Location: The trail begins from the Old Faithful Snow Lodge.

Description: Follow the Mallard Lake/Lone Star Geyser trails as they leave the Snow Lodge. Ski around the Old Faithful cabins to the Firehole River. Cross the river on the footbridge.

The trail forks here. Go left, pulling away from the river. The trail takes you into timber burned during the fires of 1988, and then past the Pipeline Group of fumaroles. The steaming pots are beautiful and intriguing, but don't ski off the trail. The ground is soft around them and the water deathly hot.

Here the trail begins a steep climb up the first of a series of plateaus. On top, you cross gently rolling terrain. The blackened "dog hair" lodgepole pine are in stark contrast to the white snow. Much of this trail is through stands of burned trees.

As you near the lake, the trail takes you around the left side of a canyon. Here the trail is narrow and steep. Near the head of the canyon, the trail passes a field of boulders and then goes through a pass to the unburned country on the other side. Once through the pass, you're in the Mallard Lake drainage.

The trail rolls past small meadows with occasional climbs. At 3.2 miles, a sign indicates the junction of Mallard Lake and Mallard Creek trails. Go left.

The trail climbs for about a mile. The view is incredible. From here, the next 2 miles are downhill, starting gently but becoming quite steep. As the terrain gets steeper, the turns get sharper. Be prepared. This is where icy conditions make skiing dicey.

The trail crosses Mallard Creek, climbs out of the drainage, and then drops another 0.9 mile to a trail junction. The right fork of this junction takes you to the Fairy Falls trailhead, 0.25 away. Stay left to return to Old Faithful.

From here, the trail parallels the Madison Junction-Old Faithful snow road for approximately 2 miles to a junction with the Biscuit Basin Trail. Along this section, the trail crosses rolling, forested terrain along a powerline corridor.

From the Biscuit Basin Trail junction it is another 2.25 miles to the Old Faithful Visitor Center. A description of the Biscuit Basin Trail is in this chapter.

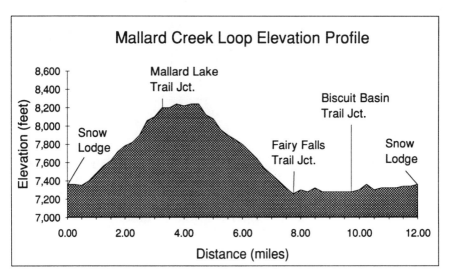

Additional Information: Call the National Park Service at 307-344-2109 (visitor information), or 307-344-7381 (central switchboard). Or write P.O. Box 168, Yellowstone National Park, Wyoming, 82190.

This trail is covered by the U.S. Geological Survey topographical maps:
Old Faithful Quadrangle, WY, 7.5 minute series
Lower Geyser Basin Quadrangle, WY, 7.5 minute series

Brimstone/Buffalo River Trails
General Overview

Sunny skies and fresh powder snow are trademarks of this neighborhood. (Photo by Ken Olsen.)

The Brimstone and Buffalo River Trail system offers 17 miles of groomed trails near Island Park, Idaho, 27 miles from West Yellowstone, Montana.

The eight trails in the group vary considerably, from the level, short Buffalo River Trail to longer, more challenging trails along Thurmon Ridge and the Henrys Fork River.

The area has great snow—as much as 6 feet by New Year's Day. Moose are common around Island Park. Other wildlife—elk, deer, bald eagles, geese and the Trumpeter Swan—share these trails in winter.

Trails are maintained as part of the Idaho Park and Ski system. Opening and closing dates depend on weather, but the snow season is usually from October to May.

To reach the Brimstone/Buffalo trails, travel west on U.S. Highway 20 from West Yellowstone, Montana, toward Island Park and Ashton, Idaho. This two-lane paved highway is fairly well-maintained in all types of weather. You will cross the continental divide about 10 miles from West Yellowstone and drop down into a broad valley. Stay on the highway past Mack's Inn and Elk Creek Station. A few miles farther, on the right, watch for Pond's Lodge.

Just beyond the lodge and the main parking lot is a small skiers' parking area near the Buffalo River. If you cross the river, you have gone too far.

You can buy Idaho state Park-and-Ski passes at Pond's Lodge. The annual pass costs $15 and is good for a year. Fees go to ski trail maintenance. If there isn't enough parking near the trailhead, cross the river and park in front of the Island Park Ranger Station, just down the road.

Pond's Lodge is open year-round. It has a restaurant, bar, lodging and two warm wood stoves.

Brimstone/Buffalo River Trails

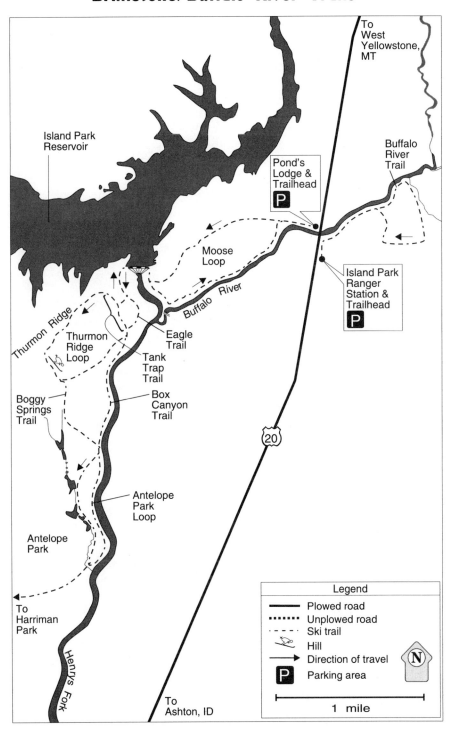

To
West
Yellowstone,
MT

Island Park
Reservoir

Buffalo
River
Trail

Pond's
Lodge &
Trailhead
P

Moose
Loop

Island Park
Ranger
Station &
Trailhead
P

Buffalo   River

Thurmon Ridge

Thurmon
Ridge
Loop

Eagle
Trail

Tank
Trap
Trail

Box
Canyon
Trail

Boggy
Springs
Trail

20

Antelope
Park
Loop

Antelope
Park

To
Harriman
Park

Henry's Fork

Legend

——	Plowed road
•••••••	Unplowed road
– – –	Ski trail
	Hill
→	Direction of travel
P	Parking area

N

1 mile

To
Ashton, ID

Difficulty:	Easy

Length: 3 miles

Easy

Grooming: Weekly, depending upon snow conditions.

Fee: $15 annual Idaho Park-and-Ski pass or $25 annual Idaho State Park pass. Also available are a $2 one-time use permit and a $7.50 3-day use permit. Prices are subject to change.

Overview: This is a trail you must ski if you're in the neighborhood. It follows gentle terrain to Island Park Reservoir and returns along the Buffalo River. Count on seeing ducks and swans on the river. Moose are often in the willow thickets along the reservoir.

Location: You can reach this trail from the Buffalo River parking area near Pond's Lodge. Detailed directions are in the introduction to this chapter.

Description: Park near the north side of the Buffalo River highway bridge or at the Island Park Ranger Station, a few hundred feet down the road. Follow the ski tracks that head west from the parking area on the north side of the bridge.

This is a mostly flat trail, perfect for beginners, but with scenery and wildlife to entice more seasoned skiers. You should see swans on the river, to your left, soon after leaving the parking lot.

The trail crosses a creek and takes you to a trail registry. Then it forks. Go right.

The trail weaves in and out of mixed conifer forests. Wildlife sometimes uses the trail, and you will probably see moose tracks.

In about 1.5 miles, you'll see a snow-covered dike, part of Island Park Reservoir. The Centennial Mountains, part of the continental divide, are a spectacular backdrop to the reservoir.

The trail turns to parallel the dike and then draws toward it. You may want to ski up on the dike and look for moose in the willow thickets.

You come to a junction. This is the far end of the loop. Eagle Trail continues across Island Park Reservoir Dam, while the Moose Loop Trail veers left.

From here, Moose Loop follows the Buffalo River upstream from its junction with the Henrys Fork. You will find a few gentle hills on this portion of the trail. Look for swans in some of the quiet tucks of the river.

As buildings come into view, slow down. A road is sometimes cut through the trail, near one of the cabins, putting two-or three-foot drop-offs in the trail.

Continue to follow the trail back to the Buffalo River parking area. Pond's Lodge offers a warm wood stove and refreshments for the weary skier.

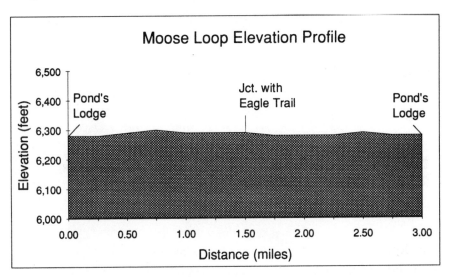

Additional Information: Call the U.S. Forest Service, Island Park Ranger Station, at 208-558-7301. Or write P.O. Box 220, Island Park, ID 83429.

This trail is covered by the U.S. Geological Survey topographical maps:
Island Park Quadrangle, ID, 7.5 minute series
Island Park Dam Quadrangle, ID, 7.5 minute series

Difficulty:	Easy	
Length:	2.6 miles	**Easy**
Grooming:	Weekly, depending upon snow conditions.	
Fee:	$15 annual Idaho Park-and-Ski pass or $25 annual Idaho State Park pass. Also available are a $2 one-time use permit and a $7.50 3-day use permit. Prices are subject to change.	
Overview:	A flat, unchallenging trail about half of which follows the Buffalo River and offers some opportunity to watch waterfowl.	
Location:	Begins in front of the Island Park Ranger Station, about 28 miles south of West Yellowstone, Montana, and less than 0.5 mile south of Pond's Lodge on U.S. Highway 20. Parking is provided in front of the ranger station on the east side of the highway.	

Description: This trail is a good choice for beginning skiers who have tried everything else the Buffalo/Brimstone trail system has to offer.

A sign on the north end of the parking lot in front of the ranger station marks the beginning of the trail. The trail runs north, paralleling the highway for a few hundred yards, before moving east (right) to a register box.

If you miss the register box or park at Pond's Lodge and come to the trail on foot, ski due east from the mile 387 sign on the highway and you will encounter the box.

The trail drops gently from the register box to the banks of the Buffalo River, and follows the river for the next 0.75 mile. For most of this stretch, the trail is within 50 feet of the river, but not right on the bank, and makes its way through lodgepole pine. The trail crosses an open meadow and drifts to the river's edge. It takes a sharp right about 0.2 mile later. Trail markers have been sparse here. Note that the trail is not so much a gentle loop as a series of gradual turns followed by sharp turns.

About 0.3 mile after turning away from the river, the trail comes to another meadow and, depending upon snow depth, the top of a rail fence. Ski directly across the pasture and into the stand of trees. Again, blue diamond markers have been sparse, but the U.S. Forest Service says it has added markers.

The trail enters a narrow lodgepole pine corridor and soon cuts right. The trail winds through the pines for several hundred yards and comes to another clearing.

Stay with the edge of the trees and watch for the trail to move to your right and head for a powerline. Because trail markers are few, you'll have to keep sharp watch if the trail has not been well-defined by groomers or skiers.

Pass under the powerline and immediately make a sharp right turn. The trail follows the powerline in a wider corridor cleared among the lodgepole. You will stay with the powerline almost until this trail rejoins the path you skied along the river.

About 0.5 mile after joining the powerline, the trail bears left. Ski a few hundred yards until you come to the river and the main trail. Turn left to ski back to the Island Park Ranger Station, about 0.5 mile away.

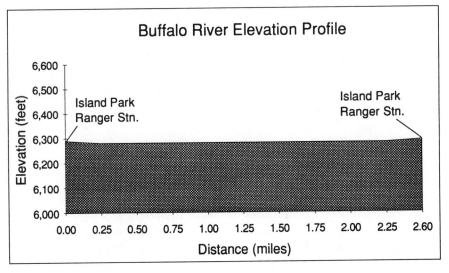

Additional Information: Call the U.S. Forest Service, Island Park Ranger Station at 208-558-7301. Or write P.O. Box 220, Island Park, ID 83429.

This trail is covered by the U.S. Geological Survey topographical map: Island Park Quadrangle, ID, 7.5 minute series

Difficulty:	Moderate	

Moderate

Length: 0.4 mile by itself, 5.5 miles round trip counting trails taken to and from the start of the Tank Trap Trail.

Grooming: Groomed weekly, depending on snow conditions, until February 28, when grooming ends to protect nesting bald eagles.

Fee: $15 annual Idaho Park-and-Ski pass or $25 annual Idaho State Park pass. Also available are a $2 one-time use permit and a $7.50 3-day use permit. Prices are subject to change.

Overview: This is an easy trail. It is rated moderate because you ski parts of Moose Loop and Eagle Trail to get to and from the Tank Trap. The trail is punctuated by road closure humps. Aside from its colorful name, this trail offers the beginner a chance to practice herringbone technique on the humps.

Location: Begins at the trailhead on the west side of Highway 20/191, just south of Pond's Lodge.

Description: From the trailhead, take Moose Loop to Eagle Trail. Follow Eagle Trail across Island Park Reservoir Dam, then up a slight rise through a clearing to the boundary of Harriman Wildlife Refuge.

Just past the boundary, the trail enters the trees and tops a hill, then begins to wind through the trees on rolling terrain. About three-fourths of the way through a moderate downhill, you meet a trail junction. The left fork is a continuation of Eagle Trail. The right fork continues on to Tank Trap Trail, 0.10 mile away.

You intersect the Tank Trap Trail midway along its length. Turning right, you will follow Tank Trap roughly 0.25 mile up moderate slopes to reach the Thurmon Ridge Loop. The trail follows an abandoned roadbed punctuated with road closure (tank trap) humps.

Turning left at the Tank Trap junction will take you to Box Canyon Trail in roughly 0.25 mile. The trail crosses level to gently rolling terrain, through open forest. The trail follows an abandoned roadbed punctuated with road closure (tank trap) humps.

Not counting connecting trails, Tank Trap is only 0.40 mile long.

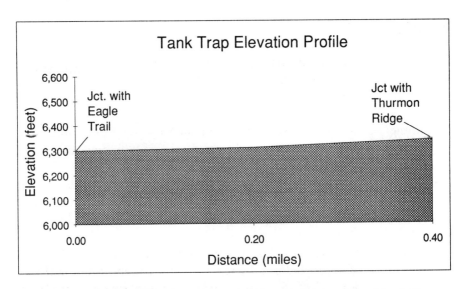

Additional Information: Call the U.S. Forest Service, Island Park Ranger Station, at 208-558-7301. Or write P.O. Box 220, Island Park, ID 83429.

This trail is covered by the U.S. Geological Survey topographical maps:
Island Park Quadrangle, ID, 7.5 minute series
Island Park Dam Quadrangle, ID, 7.5 minute series

Difficulty:	Moderate
Length:	0.6 mile by itself, 7.5 miles round trip counting trails taken to and from the start of the Boggy Springs Trail.

Moderate

Grooming: Groomed weekly, depending on snow conditions, until February 28, when grooming ends to protect nesting bald eagles.

Fee: $15 annual Idaho Park-and-Ski pass or $25 annual Idaho State Park pass. Also available are a $2 one-time use permit and a $7.50 3-day use permit. Prices are subject to change.

Overview: Boggy Springs Trail winds through quiet groves of aspen in a rolling meadow from the base of Thurmon Ridge to the Box Canyon of the Henrys Fork of the Snake River. It is one of the least-traveled trails in the Buffalo River system, but also one of the prettiest. Opportunities to see wildlife here are very good.

Location: Access this trail from the Buffalo River parking area near Pond's Lodge. Detailed directions are in the introduction to the Brimstone/Buffalo River Trails.

Description: Boggy Springs Trail is less than 1 mile long and suitable for the greenest beginner. However, to reach it you ski all or part of several other trails.

Take Moose Loop to its junction with Eagle Trail. Follow Eagle Trail to its junction with Box Canyon, then turn left and ski for 0.1 mile to the Thurmon Ridge/Box Canyon junction. Turn right onto the Thurmon Ridge Loop and follow it for roughly 0.5 mile along the base of Thurmon Ridge, until you reach the Boggy Springs Trail junction. Turn left onto Boggy Springs.

The trail begins in a mix of boulders, Douglas-fir and aspen above the springs that give this trail its name. Ski quietly and you'll likely see elk, deer, moose and bald eagles. Like all the trails on this side of Island Park Dam, Boggy Springs is in the 16,000-acre Harriman Wildlife Refuge.

As the trail wanders down to the river, the forest gradually opens up and gives way to scattered groves of aspen. At about 0.2 mile, the trail parallels a small stream that runs through Antelope Park to the river.

As you approach the Henrys Fork and the end of Boggy Springs Trail, you will see the sign for Box Canyon Trail which leads to Eagle Trail, Moose Loop and the trailhead. Antelope Loop, also on the sign, continues downstream to the farthest edge of the Buffalo River Trail System.

Harriman Wildlife Refuge is prime wintering habitat for the once-endangered Trumpeter Swans; watch for them along the river.

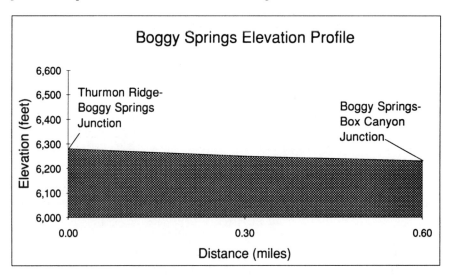

Additional Information: Call the U.S. Forest Service, Island Park Ranger Station, at 208-558-7301. Or write P.O. Box 220, Island Park, ID 83429.

This trail is covered by the U.S. Geological Survey topographical maps:
Island Park Quadrangle, ID, 7.5 minute series
Island Park Dam Quadrangle, ID, 7.5 minute series

Difficulty:	Moderate

Length: 1 mile by itself, 5 miles round trip counting trails taken to and from Eagle Trail.

Moderate

Grooming: Groomed weekly, depending on snow conditions, until February 28, when grooming ends to protect nesting bald eagles.

Fee: $15 annual Idaho Park-and-Ski pass or $25 annual Idaho State Park pass. Also available are a $2 one-time use permit and a $7.50 3-day use permit. Prices are subject to change.

Overview: This is basically a short connecting trail that links Moose Loop with all but the Buffalo River Trail. It takes you across Island Park Dam, which is a scenic vantage on a clear day.

Location: The trail begins on the west side of U.S. Highway 20, just south of Pond's Lodge.

Description: From the trailhead, take Moose Loop (see earlier in this chapter for a description of Moose Loop) almost to Island Park Dam. Eagle Trail begins at the farthest point of the Moose Loop.

As you draw near the dike that is part of the dam, take a sharp right turn, ski up a gentle incline and turn left. The trail crosses Island Park Dam. From the top of the dam, you can look down into willow thickets along the reservoir shore, a favorite spot of moose.

Eagle Trail continues across the dam, then up a slight rise through a clearing to the boundary of Harriman Wildlife Refuge. The refuge is home to moose, elk, fox, geese and the rare Trumpeter Swan. Snowmobiling is not permitted in the refuge.

Just past the boundary, the trail enters the trees and tops a hill, then begins to wind through the trees on rolling terrain. About three-fourths of the way through a moderate downhill, you meet a trail junction. The right fork continues on to Tank Trap Trail. Take a hard left to stay with Eagle Trail.

The trail makes a wide arc toward the Henrys Fork across rolling, forested terrain. At about 0.75 mile, the trail makes a slow, 90-degree right turn. It continues through the trees to a junction with the Tank Trap and Box Canyon trails, about 0.25 mile away.

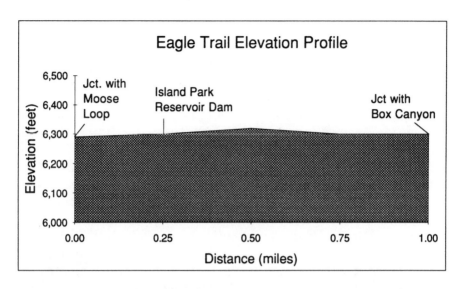

Additional Information: Call the U.S. Forest Service, Island Park Ranger Station at 208-558-7301. Or write P.O. Box 220, Island Park, ID 83429.

This trail is covered by the U.S. Geological Survey topographical maps:
Island Park Quadrangle, ID, 7.5 minute series
Island Park Dam Quadrangle, ID, 7.5 minute series

Box Canyon

Difficulty:	Moderate

Moderate

Length: 0.8 mile by itself, 6.5 miles round trip counting trails taken to and from the start of the Box Canyon trail

Grooming: Groomed weekly, depending on snow conditions, until February 28, when grooming ends to protect nesting bald eagles.

Fee: $15 annual Idaho Park-and-Ski pass or $25 annual Idaho State Park pass. Also available are a $2 one-time use permit and a $7.50 3-day use permit. Prices are subject to change.

Overview: This short, easy trail takes you along the rim of the Box Canyon of the Henrys Fork of the Snake River. It runs through Harriman Wildlife Refuge, prime winter habitat for the once-endangered Trumpeter Swan. Box Canyon Trail is 0.8 mile long, but to reach it, you also ski Moose Loop and Eagle Trail.

Location: Access is from the Buffalo River trailhead near Pond's Lodge. Detailed directions to the trailhead are in the introduction to the Brimstone/Buffalo River Trails.

Description: Box Canyon Trail is less than 1 mile long, but to reach it you ski all or part of several other trails. It is an easy trail with very little elevation change.

Take Moose Loop to its junction with Eagle Trail. Follow Eagle Trail to its junction with Tank Trap Trail. Turn left onto the Box Canyon Trail.

The trail begins in Douglas-fir forest near the base of Thurmon Ridge. About 0.1 mile after the trail begins you'll pass a junction with the lower leg of Thurmon Ridge Loop, on your right. Soon the trail leads into more open country. On your left is the Box Canyon of the Henrys Fork, and on your right is Antelope Park, an open meadow broken by groves of aspen and scattered pines. You may see moose and their calves here.

The trail ends at the junction of Boggy Springs Trail and Antelope Park Loop.

132

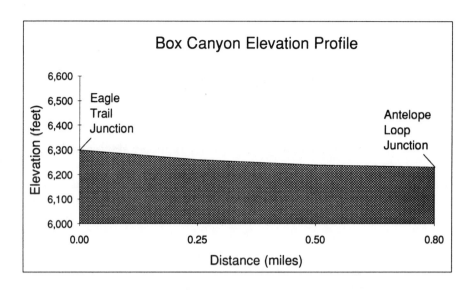

Additional Information: Call the U.S. Forest Service, Island Park Ranger Station, at 208-558-7301. Or write P.O. Box 220, Island Park, ID 83429.

This trail is covered by the U.S. Geological Survey topographical maps:
Island Park Quadrangle, ID, 7.5 minute series
Island Park Dam Quadrangle, ID, 7.5 minute series

Difficulty: Difficult

Length: 1.5 miles by itself, 7 miles round trip counting trails taken to and from the start of Thurmon Ridge Loop.

Grooming: Groomed weekly, depending on snow conditions, until February 28, when grooming ends to protect nesting bald eagles.

Fee: $15 annual Idaho Park-and-Ski pass or $25 annual Idaho State Park pass. Also available are a $2 one-time use permit and a $7.50 3-day use permit. Prices are subject to change.

Overview: This is an exciting loop to test the intermediate skier's skills. All of it is inside the Harriman Wildlife Refuge; look for swans, moose and occasional elk. The trailhead is next to Pond's Lodge where skiers can warm up next to twin wood stoves in the bar and restaurant.

Location: Access this trail from the Buffalo River parking area near Pond's Lodge. Detailed directions are in the introduction to the Brimstone/Buffalo River Trails.

Description: Through a bureaucratic bugaboo, some trail signs and maps refer to this trail as Thurburn and some call it Thurmon, the correct name of the ridge. Both refer to the same trail.

The Thurmon Ridge trail is a 1.5-mile loop, but counting access trails it's a 7-mile trip.

Take Moose Loop to its junction with Eagle Trail. Follow Eagle Trail to its junction with Tank Trap Trail. Stay to the right for Thurmon Ridge Loop.

The trail climbs gradually for about 0.75 mile through the trees across the top of this volcanic caldera. Just before the trail drops off the ridge, a yellow, triangular sign nailed on a tree warns of the 200-foot plunge.

It is possible, just past the sign, to ski off the trail and have a look below. The first 100 feet are a straight, steep drop. Then the trail winds into a narrow canyon that rushes, not quite so steeply, to the foot of the Thurmon Ridge.

Here Boggy Springs takes off to the right; it connects to Antelope Park Loop and Box Canyon Trail. The trail continues through a tumble of boulders and Douglas-fir along the base of the ridge, until the trail joins Box Canyon. Stay left to return to Eagle Trail. A little further a sign points out the Tank Trap Trail. Choose Eagle Trail and avoid climbing road-closure humps on the Tank Trap.

Eagle Trail takes you back to Moose Loop and Pond's Lodge where the Bloody Marys come highly recommended.

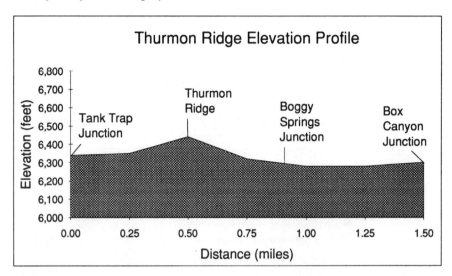

Additional Information: Call the U.S. Forest Service, Island Park Ranger Station, at 208-558-7301. Or write P.O. Box 220, Island Park, ID 83429.

This trail is covered by the U.S. Geological Survey topographical maps:
Island Park Quadrangle, ID, 7.5 minute series
Island Park Dam Quadrangle, ID, 7.5 minute series.

Difficulty: Difficult

Length: 1.6 miles by itself, 8.9 miles round trip counting trails taken to and from the start of the Antelope Park Trail.

Difficult

Grooming: Groomed weekly, depending on snow conditions, until February 28, when grooming ends to protect nesting bald eagles.

Fee: $15 annual Idaho Park-and-Ski pass or $25 annual Idaho State Park pass. Also available are a $2 one-time use permit and a $7.50 3-day use permit. Prices are subject to change.

Overview: This is an easy trail that only receives a difficult rating because—counting Moose Loop, Eagle and Box Canyon access trails—you end up skiing almost 9 miles. It runs between the rolling meadows of Antelope Park and the Henrys Fork of the Snake River, a prime wintering area for the Trumpeter Swan. This is a fairly popular trail, but still offers plenty of solitude.

Location: Access is from the Buffalo River parking area near Pond's Lodge. Detailed directions are in the introduction to the Brimstone/Buffalo River Trails.

Description: From the trailhead take Moose Loop to Eagle Trail. From Eagle, take the Box Canyon Trail to the start of Antelope Loop. Antelope Park Loop begins in open meadows along the Henrys Fork of the Snake River. The aspen-covered meadows are unlike the lodgepole pine forests that dominate many of the trails in the West Yellowstone area. The entire loop is within the Harriman Wildlife Refuge, haven to moose, elk, deer and a variety of waterfowl.

The trail forks soon after it begins. Both forks are part of Antelope Loop, but take the right one west and south into Antelope Park, an area laced with animal tracks.

At the western edge of the loop, the trail skirts a small stream fed by several springs at the foot of Thurmon Ridge. The trail turns south as it meets the stream, and follows it back to the river—and the farthest point from the trailhead. About 100 feet south of this point is a small waterfall and a popular lunch spot.

From its southernmost point, the trail turns north and takes you back along the Henrys Fork to the beginning of the loop.

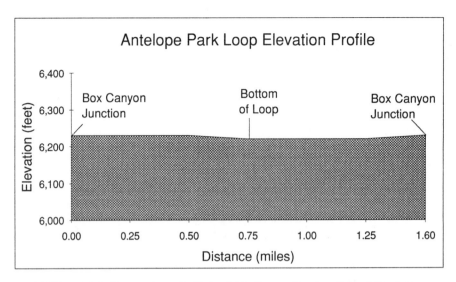

Additional Information: Call the U.S. Forest Service, Island Park Ranger Station at 208-558-7301. Or write P.O. Box 220, Island Park, ID 83429.

This trail is covered by the U.S. Geological Survey topographical maps:
Island Park Quadrangle, ID, 7.5 minute series
Island Park Dam Quadrangle, ID, 7.5 minute series

Editor's Note: The U.S. Forest Service announced this trail was being added just as this guide was going to press. This description is strictly based upon information provided by the U.S. Forest Service. Check at the Island Park Ranger Station or Harriman State Park headquarters before skiing this trail. No elevation profile or map is provided for this trail.

Difficulty:	Difficult
Length:	5.5 miles by itself, 12 miles one way counting the trails you ski to access this trail.
Grooming:	Groomed weekly, depending on snow conditions, until February 28, when grooming ends to protect nesting bald eagles.
Fee:	$15 annual Idaho Park-and-Ski pass or $25 annual Idaho State Park pass. Also available are a $2 one-time use permit and a $7.50 3-day use permit. Prices are subject to change.
Overview:	This long, beautiful ski trail connects the Antelope Loop with the Harriman State Park ski trail system. It is rated extreme because of the distance. Moose, swans and coyotes are frequently seen here, along with great views of the Henrys Fork and the Teton Range.
Location:	You can reach this trail from the Buffalo River parking area near Pond's Lodge. Detailed directions are in the introduction to this chapter. You also can reach this trail from Harriman State Park. See chapter 9 for directions to Harriman State Park.

Difficult

Description: The Brimstone-Harriman Trail is about 5.5 miles long. However, to reach it you must either ski the Moose Loop, Eagle, Box Canyon and Antelope trails, or the Moose Loop, Thurmon Ridge, Boggy Springs and Antelope trails. (See elsewhere in this chapter for information on these trails.) You can also reach the trail from Harriman State Park. See chapter 9 for directions to Harriman State Park.

From the southern tip of Antelope Loop, roughly 4.5 miles from the trailhead, you cross a small creek and ski southwest for about 0.25 mile through open aspen and lodgepole pine stands. The trail turns due west and follows a fence through a large meadow with great views of the Teton Range. You cross two creeks on snow bridges before returning to the trees in approximately 0.75 mile.

The trail continues to follow the fence line through timber for about 0.4 mile before emerging into another meadow. Turn left (south), skirting the edge of the meadow, until you reach a road.

This road follows the fence south to another meadow and continues to the Big Bend of the Henrys Fork, approximately 1 mile away. From the Big Bend you turn right (southwest) and ski in open country, with great views of the Henrys Fork and the Tetons.

You will follow fence lines and power lines for about 2 miles to the northern end of the Harriman State Park trail system. Continue south to reach the Harriman Park Railroad Ranch historical site in 0.5 mile, and Harriman State Park headquarters in 1.75 miles.

Additional Information: Call the U.S. Forest Service, Island Park Ranger Station, at 208-558-7301. Or write P.O. Box 220, Island Park, ID 83429.

This trail is covered by the U.S. Geological Survey topographical maps:
Island Park Quadrangle, ID, 7.5 minute series
Island Park Dam Quadrangle, ID, 7.5 minute series
Last Chance Quadrangle, ID, 7.5 minute series

Harriman State Park Ski Trails
General Overview

On a clear day, the Ridge Loop offers a spectacular view of the Teton Range. (Photo Ken Olsen.)

Harriman State Park, about 35 miles southwest of West Yellowstone, Montana, on U.S. Highway 20, offers 10 miles of trails—six loops—with excellent skiing for skiers of every skill level. Half of the trails are groomed at least once a week or more often if there is sufficient fresh snow.

These trails lead you through a tour of the historic Railroad Ranch, as well as taking you 9 miles into the Harriman Wildlife Refuge. Outside of the Old Faithful area, you won't find a better place to see wildlife. (Harriman Wildlife Refuge includes the 4,700-acre Harriman Ranch and 11,000 acres of U.S. Forest Service land.) Trumpeter Swans are plentiful. Moose are occasionally near the trail. Elk, deer, bald eagles, ducks, geese and other wildlife are abundant, depending on when you visit.

The official winter season is from Thanksgiving to April, but skiing is possible from October through May given the right weather. One of Idaho's newest state parks, Harriman has an average of three feet of snow by Christmas, increasing to six feet by late January.

Only 5,000 to 6,000 visitors use this area each winter, though the number is growing. The peak time for skiers is the week after Christmas. Except for the annual free skiing day, you are not likely to feel crowded here.

Park headquarters—the building near the parking lot—offers clean restrooms and helpful rangers, and sells hot drinks and books about the area.

One caution: stay off Silver Lake. Though it may be tempting to take a short cut across the glittering ice, the potential time saved is not worth the risk. The ice of Silver Lake is pocked with thin spots caused by underwater currents and hot springs. Don't risk your life to save a mile.

Harriman State Park Trails

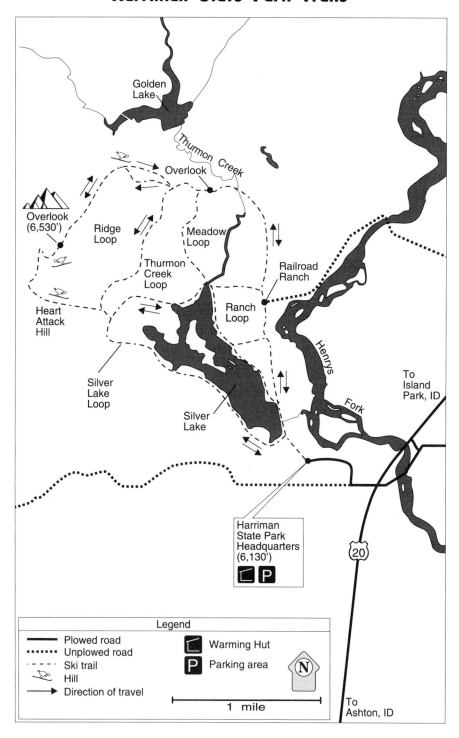

Difficulty:	Easy

Easy

Length: 2.8 miles round trip from Harriman State Park Headquarters

Grooming: Machine-groomed weekly for track skiing. The portion from park headquarters to Railroad Ranch also is groomed for skate-style skiing.

Fee: $15 annual Idaho Park-and-Ski pass or $25 annual Idaho State Park pass. Also available are a $2 one-time use permit and a $7.50 3-day use permit. Prices are subject to change.

Overview: The main buildings of the old Railroad Ranch provide a historic backdrop for this flat, easy loop. The Jones House Warming Hut opens at Christmas and offers hot drinks, tables and a fire to warm up by, but **it is open only on weekends.** You can see the Henrys Fork River and plenty of wildlife from this trail.

Location: Follows the main trail north from Harriman State Park Headquarters buildings and loops back via the east shore of Silver Lake.

Description: This easy, level trail takes off on the wide, well-groomed trail that begins at the parking lot of Harriman State Park headquarters. Head north from the parking lot, staying to the right side of the trail. Silver Lake will appear on your left within 0.25 mile, buried under snow and ice.

Stay on the main trail. Watch for muskrat, rabbits and other wildlife. Waterfowl frequent the Henrys Fork River, which meanders toward the trail. It is to your right.

In about 1 mile, the trail takes you to the old buildings that were headquarters for the Railroad Ranch. Signs tell what each building was used for when this was a work ranch. On weekends you'll see smoke rolling out of the Jones House Warming Hut chimney and into the crisp Idaho sky.

Soon after leaving the main cluster of buildings, the trail reaches a junction. To stay with the Ranch Loop, turn left (west) and ski about 0.3 mile to a trail junction at the northern tip of Silver Lake. Turn left (south) and follow the northeast shore of Silver Lake for about 0.5 mile to a third junction.

Here you have the option of turning left and taking a 0.25 mile branch that leads back to the main trail. Or keep heading south, along the lake, and you will intersect the main trail in another 0.5 mile.

In either case, when you come to the main trail, turn right (south) to return to the parking lot and Harriman State Park Headquarters.

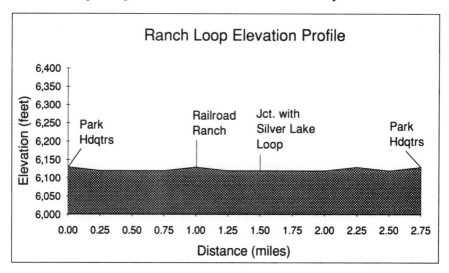

Additional Information: Contact Harriman State Park at 208-558-7368 or HC-66, Box 500, Island Park, ID 83429.

This trail is covered by the U.S. Geological Survey topographical map: Last Chance Quadrangle, ID, 7.5 minute series

Difficulty: Easy

Length: 4.2 miles round trip from Harriman State Park Headquarters

Easy

Grooming: Machine groomed weekly for track skiing. The portion from park headquarters to Thurmon Creek Overlook is also groomed for skate-style skiing.

Fee: $15 annual Idaho Park-and-Ski pass or $25 annual Idaho State Park pass. Also available are a $2 one-time use permit and a $7.50 3-day use permit. Prices are subject to change.

Overview: This is a pleasant continuation of the Ranch Loop with mostly level terrain on a well-groomed trail. The trail passes the Jones House Warming Hut, which offers a pleasant fire and sells hot drinks. **But it is open only on the weekends, beginning at Christmas.** The skiing is not particularly challenging—though there are some gentle hills—but the views are grand. On a clear day, you can see the Teton Range from part of this loop.

Location: Begins at Harriman State Park Headquarters, heading north through the old ranch buildings, loops through a meadow and returns via a lodgepole pine stand and Silver Lake.

Description: Follow the wide, well-groomed trail beginning just north of the parking lot at Harriman State Park Headquarters. Stay to the right side of the trail.

Within 0.25 mile, Silver Lake appears on your left as does the Silver Lake Trail junction. Stay with the main trail and start watching for wildlife on the Henrys Fork River, on your right. This is a great place to see waterfowl.

Approximately 1 mile from the trailhead you come to the old Railroad Ranch buildings. Signs mark each building and explain what they were used for. On weekends, beginning at Christmas, the Jones House Warming Hut sells hot drinks and offers a nice fire to warm by.

Keep skiing north from the warming hut and continue straight at the nearby junction. The trail continues out across an open meadow, offering pleasing views of the snow-covered expanse with mountains in the background. In about 0.5 mile the trail curves to the left and then crosses Thurmon Creek in another 0.25 mile.

You reach another junction soon after crossing Thurmon Creek, which will take you around the south side of the Thurman Creek Overlook. At this junction, the Thurmon Creek Loop heads to the right (west). To take the Meadow Loop continue straight (south) and follow the trail in and out of lodgepole pine and over gentle hills to the head of Silver Lake, about 0.75 mile later. You should be able to see the Tetons on the far horizon.

You cross Thurmon Creek on a footbridge at the head of Silver Lake. A trail junction here allows you to go left (east) and return to the Railroad Ranch. Most skiers turn right (south) along the shore of Silver Lake.

As you follow the gently rolling terrain of the Silver Lake shore, you will meet another junction in approximately 0.5 mile. The left fork of this junction leads east to the main trail. Most skiers go straight (south) at this junction to continue along the Silver Lake shore, reaching the main trail in 0.5 mile, and Harriman State Park Headquarters in another 0.25 mile.

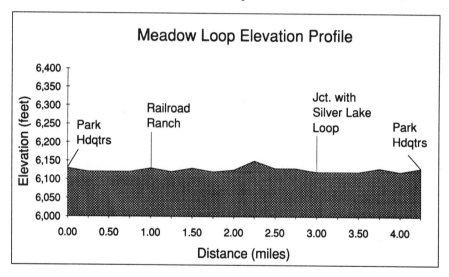

Additional Information: Contact Harriman State Park at 208-558-7368 or HC-66, Box 500, Island Park, ID 83429.

This trail is covered by the U.S. Geological Survey topographical map: Last Chance Quadrangle, ID, 7.5 minute series

Difficulty:	Moderate	

Difficulty: Moderate

Length: 4 miles round trip from Harriman State Park Headquarters

Moderate

Grooming: Ungroomed, but frequently skied.

Fee: $15 annual Idaho Park-and-Ski pass or $25 annual Idaho State Park pass. Also available are a $2 one-time use permit and a $7.50 3-day use permit. Prices are subject to change.

Overview: This moderately difficult loop provides fun skiing, with some short, steep hills and tight turns that are good places for beginners and intermediate skiers to practice. Icy conditions can make parts of the trail difficult for novice skiers. It loops around Silver Lake and much of the trail winds through lodgepole pine. The Teton Range is visible from the east side of the loop.

Location: This trail begins at Harriman State Park headquarters, leading north for 0.25 mile before turning left to circle Silver Lake clockwise.

Description: Ski about 0.25 mile north on the main, well-groomed trail that begins at Harriman State Park Headquarters. On the left, at the southern end of Silver Lake, a sign indicates the beginning of this loop. Veer left from the main trail and enter the lodgepole pine forest.

The trail winds through the trees for the next 2 miles with a nice blend of gentle downhills and a few faster, steeper hills. None are treacherous if you pay attention and watch for hummocks and corners that can trip up the inattentive skier. Take extra precautions if the trail is icy.

The steepest downhill is about 1 mile from where the Silver Lake Loop leaves the main trail. Stop before you head down and look for skiers coming from the other direction.

After this drop, the trail climbs briefly, and continues its gentle winding pattern through the trees. Two miles from the main trail, the loop comes to an open meadow, bisected by a fence that may be covered with snow.

The trail turns right, soon coming to the Ridge Loop Trail junction. Keep skiing straight ahead (northeast) to stay with the Silver Lake Loop.

The trail enters trees again and the terrain is mostly level, with an occasional gentle bump or slight hill. It leads northeast, east, then northeast and hits the northern tip of Silver Lake in about 0.5 mile, crossing Thurmon Creek on a footbridge. The Grand Teton Mountains are visible to the south. The skiing is easy and pleasant.

Just after the Thurmon Creek crossing, a trail junction allows you to veer left (east) to the Railroad Ranch, or turn right (south) along the shore of Silver Lake. Continuing along Silver Lake takes you across gently rolling terrain to another trail junction in 0.5 mile. Going left (east) here takes you out to the main trail. Most skiers continue straight (south) at this junction to follow the Silver Lake shoreline, reaching the main trail in 0.5 mile and Harriman State Park Headquarters in another 0.25 mile.

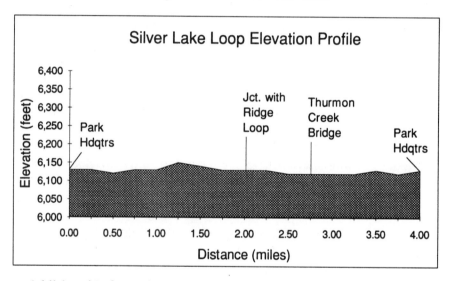

Additional Information: Contact Harriman State Park at 208-558-7368 or HC-66, Box 500, Island Park, ID 83429.

This trail is covered by the U.S. Geological Survey topographical map: Last Chance Quadrangle, ID, 7.5 minute series

Difficulty: Moderate

Length: 5.5 miles round trip from Harriman State Park Headquarters

Grooming: Tracked by skiers

Fee: $15 annual Idaho Park-and-Ski pass or $25 annual Idaho State Park pass. Also available are a $2 one-time use permit and a $7.50 3-day use permit. Prices are subject to change.

Overview: This is a pleasant loop that takes you to the Thurmon Creek overlook via the Silver Lake Trail and an old logging road. From the overlook you can see the Tetons, the Centennial Mountains, waterfowl and occasionally wildlife.

Location: This trail begins at Harriman State Park Headquarters, heading north for 0.25 mile to the Silver Lake Junction. It follows the Silver Lake trail around the west side of Silver Lake, then proceeds north to the Thurmon Creek overlook. It then joins the Meadow Loop Trail to return along the eastern shore of Silver Lake.

Description: Ski about 0.25 mile north on the main, well-groomed trail that begins at Harriman State Park Headquarters. On the left, at the southern end of Silver Lake, a sign indicates the beginning of the Silver Lake Loop Trail. Veer left onto the Silver Lake Loop Trail and enter the lodgepole pine forest.

The trail winds through the trees for the next 2 miles with a nice blend of gentle downhills and a few faster, steeper hills. None are treacherous if you pay attention and watch for hummocks and corners that can trip up the inattentive skier. Take extra precautions if the trail is icy.

The trail dips down, heads up a short, steep hill and continues its gentle winding pattern through the trees. Two miles from the main trail, the loop comes to an open meadow, bisected by a fence that may be covered by snow.

The tracks turn right, soon meeting the Ridge Loop junction. As the sign indicates, you go left, skiing up a gentle hill. Watch for skiers coming down the hill. Yield to them.

Soon the trail forks again. Go right, staying the gentle uphill course. This area has been logged and you are following the switchbacks of an old logging road. Just over 1 mile of rolling topography brings you to the northern-most point of the trail. The Ridge Loop Trail takes off to the left, so bear right to continue skiing the Thurmon Creek Loop.

Another junction soon appears. Turn left (north). The trail gently turns east, taking you to the Thurmon Creek Overlook. From the overlook you get a good view of the Tetons and the Centennial Mountains. To stay with the Thurmon Creek Loop, turn right at the next junction and on to the Meadow Loop Trail.

Follow the trail in and out of lodgepole pines and over gentle hills to the head of Silver Lake, about 0.75 mile later. You should be able to see the Tetons on the far horizon.

At the head of Silver Lake you cross Thurmon Creek on a footbridge. Just beyond the crossing, a trail junction allows you to veer left (east) to the Railroad Ranch or turn right (south) along the shore of Silver Lake. Continuing along Silver Lake takes you across gently rolling terrain to another trail junction in 0.5 mile. Going left (east) here takes you out to the main trail. Most skiers continue straight (south) at this junction to follow the Silver Lake shoreline, reaching the main trail in 0.5 mile, and Harriman State Park Headquarters in another 0.25 mile.

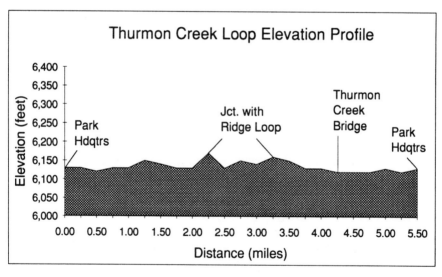

Additional Information: Contact Harriman State Park at 208-558-7368 or HC-66, Box 500, Island Park, ID 83429.

This trail is covered by the U.S. Geological Survey topographical map: Last Chance Quadrangle, ID, 7.5 minute series Ridge Loop

Difficulty: Difficulty

Length: 8 miles

Difficult

Grooming: None, but rangers try to set tracks regularly.

Fee: $15 annual Idaho Park-and-Ski pass or $25 annual Idaho State Park pass. Also available are a $2 one-time use permit and a $7.50 3-day use permit. Prices are subject to change.

Overview: This is a fun trail. It is challenging for the intermediate skier with its climb and descent of about 400 feet in less than 2 miles. From the top, skiers are guaranteed a stunning view of the Teton Range (weather permitting), and are likely to be rewarded by close encounters with moose. This trail is home to Heart Attack Hill and Coronary Bypass. It offers some of the best skiing on this side of the park.

Location: From the Harriman State Park headquarters you'll follow a broad trail groomed for both skate and stride skiers. In sight of Silver Lake, a trail takes off to the left. This trail (Silver Lake Loop) runs along the south side of the lake and leads to the Ridge Loop.

Description: The Ridge Loop follows the Thurmon Loop trail for its first 3.25 miles to the northern junction of the Ridge Loop and Thurman Creek Loop. (See elsewhere in this chapter for a discussion of the Thurmon Creek Loop.) Turn left (west) at this junction onto the Ridge Loop.

As the trail leads you out of the logged area and back into pines, you pass a trail to the left marked "do not enter." Believe it. Skiers come down the tight curves from Thurmon Ridge very fast here. Go a little farther to the uphill trail. Here you quickly move into rocky, forested terrain.

The first 0.75 mile climbs steeply, but for the most part, you don't have to herringbone. The last 0.25 mile is very steep and often requires you to herringbone and sidestep. The trail is often icy here, too. By way of compensation, the aspen groves are lovely.

From the top, the trail takes off to the southwest along the edge of the ridge. About midway, the trail brings you to a sunny opening in the pines. The view of the Tetons and the park from here is magnificent.

Soon after you leave the overlook, the trail begins to drop back off the ridge. The first steep drop takes off to the right through aspen and pine, and ends in a 90-degree turn at the edge of a clearing. From here, the trail picks up another logging road and descends gently for about 0.5 mile before leaving the road and quickly descending a tight draw.

The trail levels again, briefly, as you meander through a narrow valley on the lower ridge.

The valley leads to the top of Heart Attack Hill, a fast, straight drop that can be a little icy. The heart attack factor applies mainly to those poor souls who have to climb the hill, rather than those who take it down the ridge. For travelers in either direction, it can be bypassed. The well-named Coronary Bypass is marked at the top of Heart Attack Hill, but is often not tracked. The bypass follows a very gentle route.

Heart Attack Hill ends in a pretty little meadow. From here, the trail stays in timber and crosses a series of small hills before the final, easy descent from the ridge brings you back to the west end of Silver Lake.

From here you follow the Silver Lake Loop to either the left or right to take you around Silver Lake and back to the Harriman State Park Headquarters. (See elsewhere in this chapter for a description of the Silver Lake Loop.)

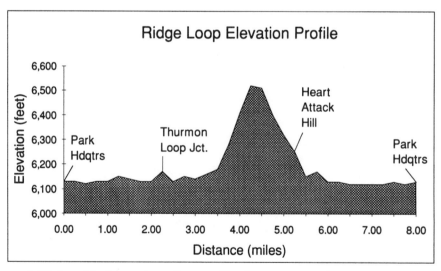

Additional Information: Contact Harriman State Park at 208-558-7368 or HC-66, Box 500, Island Park, ID 83429.

This trail is covered by the U.S. Geological Survey topographical map: Last Chance Quadrangle, ID, 7.5 minute series

Personal Favorites

You can find whatever kind of skiing you're looking for in the Yellowstone area. The variety is limitless, ranging from remote backcountry trails to groomed lanes for skate-style skiing. It's risky to recommend any one trail, given the unpredictability of snow, weather and wildlife. At the risk of shortchanging all other trails we make these recommendations of trails to match your mood. The recommendations are based on our experiences with the trails over the past several years. Full trail descriptions are found elsewhere in this book, and the page number appears at the end of each description.

For those lazy days:

If you're staying in West Yellowstone and want to take a leisurely ski without the bother and expense of traveling to a distant trail, you have two excellent possibilities:

Riverside Ski Trail:
The Riverside trailhead is just off Boundary Street in West Yellowstone, an easy walk from most any motel in town.

The Riverside Trail is easy, with a few moderately difficult hills. There is excellent scenery along both the upriver and downriver loops, which parallel the Madison River. Wildlife is present but not abundant. (See trail description beginning on page 73.)

Rendezvous Ski Trail:
The Rendezvous Ski Trail system starts just off Yellowstone Street in West Yellowstone, within easy walking distance of most West Yellowstone motels.

The many loops and cutoffs on the Rendezvous Ski Trail system allow for route combinations from a few miles to 15 miles. The trails are easy to moderately difficult. (See trail description beginning on page 77.)

Upper Terrace Loop:
This 1.5-mile loop is one of the most accessible trails in northern Yellowstone National Park. It follows the Upper Terrace road around White Elephant Back Terrace and other beautiful thermal features just south of the Mammoth Hot Springs Motor Inn. You are likely to see wintering elk and deer as well as spectacular scenery. This trail is moderately difficult (See trail description beginning on page 24.)

Black Sand Basin:
Found in the heart of Yellowstone National Park, near Old Faithful, this 4.25-mile trail is easy skiing on level terrain. It takes you past the Firehole River and a variety of beautiful thermal features including Black Sand Pool. (See trail description beginning on page 94.)

For a trail less traveled by:

If you want to get off the beaten path and don't mind skiing unmaintained trails, we offer the following suggestions:

Campanula Springs Ski Trail:
The Campanula Springs trailhead is 9 miles north of West Yellowstone on Highway 191.

The Campanula Springs Trail is easy, with the exception of a steep, difficult downhill run through the trees at the trail's end. The trail is ungroomed, but it is rare to find it unskied. You'll see panoramic views of the Richards Creek drainage. (See trail description beginning on page 57.)

Wildlife viewing:

For both abundance and variety of wildlife, a trip into Yellowstone National Park is unbeatable. Because not everyone can afford the time and expense of getting into the park we offer alternatives both inside and outside the park.

Biscuit Basin Ski Trail:
The Biscuit Basin Ski Trail starts at the Old Faithful Visitor Center in Yellowstone National Park. Access to Old Faithful is by over-snow vehicle only. Information on transportation is in the front of this guide, beginning on page 12.

The Biscuit Basin Trail is of moderate difficulty because of its length and a few minor hills. It is a popular trail, so don't expect to find peace, solitude and pristine ski trails. However, this is the place for spectacular scenery and abundant wildlife. (See trail description beginning on page 98.)

Antelope Park Loop Ski Trail:
The Antelope Park Loop Ski Trail starts at Pond's Lodge, Island Park, Idaho, approximately 30 miles south of West Yellowstone on Highway 20.

We've rated the trail difficult because it has some moderately challenging hills, and because it is relatively long–7.5 miles or more, depending on which approach trail you choose. The trail skirts the Henrys Fork River as it flows out of Island Park Reservoir. Ducks, geese and swans are almost always seen on both the Henrys Fork and Buffalo rivers. Moose and, to a lesser extent, elk are also here. (See trail description beginning on page 136.)

Skate-style skiing:

If you're into skate-style cross-country skiing, West Yellowstone has a world-class trail system waiting for you:

Rendezvous Ski Trail:
The Rendezvous Ski Trail system starts just off Yellowstone Street in West Yellowstone.

The many loops and cutoffs on the Rendezvous Ski Trail system allow for a great number of route combinations ranging in length from a few miles to 15 miles. The trails are easy to moderately difficult. The Rendezvous trails are groomed daily to provide a 12-foot wide lane for skate-style skiing and a single track for classic "diagonal" skiing. (See trail description beginning on page 77.)

Scenery:

There isn't a single mile of ski trail in Yellowstone country that is ugly. But some areas are more stunning than others. They include:

Biscuit Basin Trail:
This trail begins near the Old Faithful Visitor Center and carries a moderate rating. The terrain is easy and the variety of wildlife is unmatched. In addition, this trail takes you past several thermal features including Morning Glory Pool. (See trail description beginning on page 98.)

Divide Trail:
Divide Lookout climbs to the Continental Divide, affording spectacular views of the central portion of Yellowstone National Park, including Shoshone Lake. The fire lookout was removed in 1991. The trail is rated difficult. (See trail description beginning on page 110.)

Blacktail Plateau Trail:
Located in northern Yellowstone National Park, near Tower Junction, this is a pleasant 8-mile journey with grand views of area mountain ranges and some great downhill runs. Elk, coyote and deer frequent the area. This trail is rated difficult because the downhill sections are challenging when hard-packed or icy. (See trail description beginning on page 41.)

Challenge:

Bunsen Peak Trail:

This 6-mile trail includes 3 miles of challenging downhill switchbacks, beginning a few miles from Mammoth Hot Springs.

It should only be attempted when groomed or after a fresh snow. When icy, it will be treacherous for even the most experienced skiers. Inquire at the Mammoth Visitor Center before venturing off on this trail. (See trail description beginning on page 29.)

Divide Trail:

This trail includes exhilarating downhill stretches from the top of the Continental Divide, in central Yellowstone Park. It begins about 7 miles from Old Faithful.

Because this trail climbs to the top of the divide, it has grand views of the park and of Shoshone Lake, the second largest in the park. (See trail description beginning on page 110.)

Thurmon Ridge Trail:

This is an exciting loop to test the intermediate skier's skills. Thurmon Ridge Loop is part of the Buffalo River trail system that begins at Island Park 27 miles southwest of West Yellowstone.

Although this trail is described as a 2.5-mile loop in the Forest Service maps available just beyond the trailhead, you ski the Moose Loop and part of Eagle Trail getting to and from Thurmon Ridge. All together, it's a 5.5-mile trip.

The Thurmon Trail climbs through trees across the top of a ridge. At the southernmost point of the loop, the trail plunges 200 feet off Thurmon Ridge. (See trail description beginning on page 134.)

Ridge Loop:

Part of the Harriman State Park Trail system, the Ridge Loop includes both variety and challenge. Much of it is not groomed, but is frequently skied so you are not likely to be breaking new snow. One portion of the trail is extremely steep, requiring you to herringbone up the slope. From the top of the ridge, you will have a spectacular view of the Teton Range. Coming down, Heart Attack Hill or Coronary Bypass will get your blood pumping. (See trail description beginning on page 151.)

Telemark skiing:

Fir Ridge Trail:
The Fir Ridge/Campanula Springs Trail will take you within sight of Sandy Butte with broad, open slopes that are great for telemark practice. In addition, this area about 9 miles north of West Yellowstone, Montana, sits above Richards Creek. The drainage is frequented by elk, buffalo and coyote. (See trail description beginning on page 57.)

Bunsen Peak Trail:
The slopes of Bunsen Peak, in northern Yellowstone near Mammoth Hot Springs, also are great for telemark skiing. If conditions aren't right for doing the entire trail, or if you don't want to tackle the challenging downhill turns on the last 3 miles of the trail, consider skiing the 3 miles to the base of the peak and playing on its slopes. (See trail description beginning on page 29.)

Snow Pass Trail:
This trail also is in northern Yellowstone National Park. If you want to telemark, you might consider starting at the Rustic Falls end of the trail. This will take you around Terrace Mountain, which slopes down to the trail. These slopes are perfect for telemarking practice. Unless you are confident of your ability to handle extreme downhill turns, return to the Rustic Falls entrance instead of trying to ski the entire trail. (See trail description beginning on page 26.)

Washburn Hills:
The Washburn Hills area is 4 miles north of Canyon at the Washburn Hot Springs Overlook. Access to this area is by over-snow vehicle only.

This is an unmaintained area providing backcountry skiing on steep, open hillsides for the advanced skier. This is **not** an area for novice skiers.

Avalanche danger can be high. Be sure to check with a ranger at the Canyon Warming Hut concerning local snow conditions. It is recommended that you not ski this area alone, and that you leave information with a friend concerning your planned route and return time. Avalanche transmitters and climbing skins are strongly advised. (See trail description beginning on page 69.)

Lodging, Additional Information

Accommodations in Yellowstone National Park

Within Yellowstone National Park, there are only two lodging facilities available during winter—Old Faithful Snow Lodge and the Mammoth Motor Inn. Both are operated by TW Recreational Services, Inc.

Room rates are not included because they change every season. If you're thinking of reserving a room at either of these locations you should call early; these facilities are booked months in advance. You should make reservation inquiries well before August.

Old Faithful Snow Lodge, Yellowstone National Park:

Operators:	TW Recreational Services, Inc. Yellowstone National Park, WY 82190 (307) 344-7311
Winter season:	Mid-December to mid-March. This may vary with weather and snow conditions.
Winter access:	Accessible by over-snow travel only from approximately December 15 to March 20 (may vary with weather and snow conditions). 30 miles from West Yellowstone, Montana; 51 miles from Mammoth Hot Springs, Wyoming; 43 miles from Flagg Ranch, Wyoming.

Mammoth Motor Inn, Yellowstone National Park:

Operators:	TW Recreational Services, Inc. Yellowstone National Park, WY 82190 (307) 344-7311
Winter season:	Mid-December to mid-March. (May vary with weather and snow conditions.)
Winter access:	Accessible by automobile year round via U.S. Highway 89 south from Livingston, Montana. Mammoth Hot Springs is 5 miles south of Gardiner, Montana.

158

For More Information

Listed below are some phone numbers and addresses you may find useful. We have tried to be accurate; however, the National Park Service was changing its telephone system as this book was going to press and some numbers may have changed. Nothing here should be construed as an endorsement of a particular business.

General Information:

Gardiner Chamber of Commerce
P.O. Box 81
Gardiner, MT 59030
(406) 848-7971

Island Park Area Chamber of Commerce
P.O. Box 83
Island Park, ID 83429

U.S. Department of the Interior
National Park Service
Yellowstone National Park, Headquarters
P.O. Box 168
Yellowstone National Park,WY 82190
Central Switchboard (307) 344-7381
Vistitor Information (307) 344-2109

West Yellowstone Chamber of Commerce
Office and Information
P.O. Box 458
100 Yellowstone Ave.
West Yellowstone, MT 59758
(406) 646-7701

Lodging in the Park:

TW Recreational Services, Inc.
Yellowstone National Park, WY 82190
(307) 344-7311

Area lodging:

Flagg Ranch
Box 187, Highway 187
Moran, WY 83013
(307) 733-8761
(800) 443-2311

Gardiner Chamber of Commerce
P.O. Box 81
Gardiner, MT 59030
(406) 848-7971

Pond's Lodge
P.O. Box 258
Island Park, ID 83429
(208) 558-7221

West Yellowstone Chamber of Commerce
Office and Information
P.O. Box 458
100 Yellowstone Ave.
West Yellowstone, MT 59758
(406) 646-7701

Ski trail information:

Harriman State Park
HC-66, Box 500
Island Park, ID 83429
(208) 558-7368

Island Park Ranger Station
P.O. Box 220
Island Park, ID 83429
(208) 558-7301

U.S. Department of the Interior
National Park Service
Yellowstone National Park, Headquarters
P.O. Box 168
Yellowstone National Park,WY 82190
Central Switchboard (307) 344-7381
Vistitor Information (307) 344-2109

Equipment sales/rentals:

Bud Lilly's Trout Shop
P.O. Box 698
39 Madison Ave.
West Yellowstone, MT 59758
(406) 646-7801

Madison River Outfitters
P.O. Box 1106
117 Canyon Street
West Yellowstone, MT 59758
(406) 646-9644

Mammoth Hot Springs Hotel
TW Recreational Services, Inc.
Yellowstone National Park, WY 82190
(307) 344-7311

Old Faithful Snow Lodge
TW Recreational Services, Inc.
Yellowstone National Park, WY 82190
(307) 344-7311

Park's Fly Shop
P.O. Box 196
Gardiner, Montana 59030
(406) 848-7314

The Cooke City Bike Shack
Highway 212
Cooke City, MT 59020
(406) 838-2412

Photography and Artwork Credits

Front cover photograph: Denver Bryan

Pen and ink drawing, title page: Robin Brown

Back cover photographs: Steve Scharosch

All other photographs as credited within the book.

Typesetting/layout provided by Document Express

Cartography by Abacus Enterprises, Inc.

About the Authors

Ken Olsen works as a daily newspaper reporter, freelance writer and photographer in Pullman, Washington. Dena Olsen is a former newspaper reporter now writing for Washington State University and the University of Idaho who loves to ski and backpack.

Steve Scharosch runs a computer consulting firm in Casper, Wyoming. Hazel Scharosch teaches at a rural Wyoming school. All of the authors have spent the last several years exploring Yellowstone National Park by skis.

List of Maps

Notes:

Notes:

Notes:

Notes: